Island Sounds in the Global City

Caribbean Popular Music and Identity in New York

EDITED BY RAY ALLEN AND LOIS WILCKEN

UNIVERSITY OF ILLINOIS PRESS
URBANA AND CHICAGO

First Illinois paperback, 2001
© 1998 by The New York Folklore Society and
The Institute for Studies in American Music, Brooklyn College
Reprinted by arrangement with the copyright holders
All rights reserved
Manufactured in the United States of America
P 5 4 3 2 1
∞ This book is printed on acid-free paper.

"Buscando Ambiente: Puerto Rican Musicians in New York City, 1917-1940" is reprinted from
My Music Is My Flag: Puerto Rican Musicians and Their New York Communities, 1917-1940
by Ruth Glassser, 1995. Reprinted with permission from the University of California Press.
"From Transplant to Transnational Circuit: Merengue in New York" is excerpted from *Meren-
gue: Dominican Music and Dominican Identity* by Paul Austerlitz, 1997. Reprinted with per-
mission from Temple University Press. "Recapturing History: The Puerto Rican Roots of Hip
Hop Culture" is excerpted from "Puerto Rocks: New York Ricans State Their Claim" by Juan
Flores in *Droppin' Science: Critical Essays on Rap Music and Hip Hop Culture,* ed. William
Eric Perkins, 1996. Reprinted with permission from Temple University Press. "Community
Dramatized, Community Contested: The Politics of Celebration in the Brooklyn Carnival" is
excerpted from *Caribbean New York: Black Immigrants and the Politics of Race* by Philip
Kasinitz, 1992. Reprinted with permission from Cornell University Press.

Library of Congress Cataloging-in-Publication Data
Island sounds in the global city : Caribbean popular music and
identity in New York / edited by Ray Allen and Lois Wilcken.
p.   cm.
Originally published: New York : New York Folklore Society : Institute for Studies in
American Music, Brooklyn College, 1998.
Includes discography (p.   ) and bibliographical references.
ISBN 0-252-07042-9 (pbk. : alk. paper)
1. Popular music—New York (State)—New York—History and criticism. 2. Popular
music—Caribbean Area—History and criticism. 3. Caribbean Americans—New York (State)—
New York—Music—History and criticism. 4. Puerto Ricans—New York (State)—
New York—Music—History and criticism. I. Title. II. Allen, Ray. III. Wilcken, Lois.
ML3477.1.I85   2001
781.64'089'6872907471—dc21   2001027820

CONTENTS

Introduction
Island Sounds in the Global City

Ray Allen and Lois Wilcken

The sounds and sights of Caribbean culture permeate New York City's diverse neighborhoods, from Manhattan's Washington Heights to Brooklyn's Crown Heights, from the barrios of the south Bronx to the streets of south Queens. In the 1990s New York City boasts the largest and most diverse concentration of Caribbean people in the world. This is not surprising, for the city has been a center of Caribbean migration since significant Puerto Rican, Cuban, and West Indian communities were established in Manhattan during the early decades of this century. The Caribbean population grew rapidly during and after World War Two with the in-migration of large numbers of Puerto Rican citizens. Following the 1965 Immigration Act, increasing numbers of Jamaicans, Trinidadians, Haitians, and Dominicans settled in central Brooklyn, the south Bronx, parts of Queens, and upper Manhattan. Today well over two million New Yorkers (approaching one-third of the city's population by many estimates) trace their lineage to the Caribbean Islands.

The "Caribbeanization" of New York, as Constance Sutton points out in *Caribbean Life in New York City* (1987, 15-30), has wrought profound changes in the city's economic, political, and cultural landscape. Moreover, New York has emerged as a Caribbean crossroads in two important respects: first, as a geographic center of interaction among peoples from different island backgrounds; and second, as a gateway between the islands and mainland America. Relatively inexpensive airfares and telecommunications links have facilitated, in Sutton's words, a "continuous and intense bi-directional flow of peoples, ideas, practices, and ideologies between the Caribbean region and New York City," and generated a "transnational, socio-cultural system" (Sutton 1987, 20).

Nowhere is this transnational crossroads phenomenon more apparent than in the realm of popular music. Internationally recognized as the center of contemporary Latin and West Indian music, New York's connections to Caribbean music reflect an ongoing process of cultural exchange that is nearly a century old. Spurred by the advent of radio, the proliferation of commercial recordings, and the immigration of influential musicians to New York City, traditional Caribbean styles became increasingly influenced by American jazz and popular music of the 1920s. Meanwhile New York had emerged as a major commercial center for recording, broadcasting, and staging performances of "ethnic" popular music. Latin themes were evident in turn-of-the-century vaudeville and popular song, and by the 1920s Trinidadian calypsonians like Wilmoth Houdini and Cuban instrumentalists like Alberto Socarras were gracing the stages of New York's theaters. In 1930 Don Azpiazu's Havana Casino Orchestra brought authentic Cuban dance music to Broadway. By the late 1930s, New York–based Afro-Cuban innovators Machito and Mario Bauza were fusing the mambo and Latin percussion with African-American big-band jazz instrumentation and swing arrangements.

Over the past thirty years, increased Caribbean migration to New York City further stimulated the musical mix. With an unparalleled network of recording companies, radio stations, and performance venues, New York City rose to prominence as a world center of Caribbean jazz and popular music. *Salsa*, based on the further blending of Cuban dance music and African-American jazz, became the primary expression of New York's "Nuyorican" (New York–born individuals of Puerto Rican heritage) culture during the 1960s and 1970s. *Soca*, a fusion of Trinidadian calypso and African-American soul, appeared in Brooklyn and Port of Spain during the 1980s, while steel bands became an integral part of Brooklyn's Labor Day Carnival celebration. Haitian *konpa* (mini-jazz) and the Dominican *merengue*, performed by electric, horn-driven ensembles, became the favored music in many New York Caribbean clubs. Younger Latin, Haitian, and West Indian players consciously continued to fuse modern jazz idioms with traditional island rhythms. Today, many prominent Caribbean players remain based in New York, where a vigorous musical interchange continues unabated.

The scholarship devoted to Caribbean music in New York has been, until recently, surprisingly thin, given the intensity and diversity of activity. Several valuable works provide an introduction to New York's Latin music scene (Roberts 1979; Boggs 1992; Glasser

1995), but the popular traditions of more recent Caribbean immigrants from the Dominican Republic, Trinidad, Jamaica, and Haiti remain unexplored, and little comparative work has been undertaken.[1] How Caribbean-New Yorkers use their musical traditions to express a sense of group identity, or to mediate intergroup tensions in the modern, multicultural urban setting, remains to be explored.

With this in mind the Institute for Studies in American Music at Brooklyn College organized a symposium focusing on the relationship of Caribbean popular music and cultural identity in New York City. Held in April of 1995, and titled "Island Sounds in the Global City," it brought together scholars, musicians, and promoters representing a broad spectrum of New York-based Caribbean styles. Highlights of the conference are presented in this volume. They reveal a rich musical landscape that is only beginning to be understood and appreciated.

Several salient themes emerge from the essays that follow. As Ruth Glasser points out in the lead article, conventional models that view urban ethnic communities as monolithic and insular, and ethnic music practices as isolated, old-country transplants, are simply not valid when applied to the experiences of New York's Puerto Rican migrants or the city's more recent Caribbean immigrants. Class, religion, region of origin, and skin color can divide any given ethnic or national group and lead to a multiplicity of musical tastes and practices. For example, issues of class and skin hue placed limitations on where and what Puerto Rican musicians could perform in New York. Class, skin color, and religious preferences, argues Lois Wilcken, all contributed to the ambivalent reception Haitian-American folkloric troupes received in New York. Ray Allen and Les Slater note that well-to-do West Indian New Yorkers often dismissed steel pan music as crude and undignified.

Noting the dynamic, fluid nature of the Caribbean-American experience, Glasser argues for an interactive approach that stresses mutual exchange of musical ideas and practices among groups. The New York-based Puerto Rican musicians she studied frequently mixed styles and repertories with Cuban-American and African-American players in uptown dance halls and downtown clubs. Juan Flores' study of the Puerto Rican contributions to New York's hip hop scene reveals a long history of cultural synthesis between the city's black and Puerto Rican peoples. While most musicians enjoyed strong support within their own community, many sought to "cross over" to wider audiences for artistic recognition and financial gain. Glasser, Allen and Slater, and Don Hill note that as early as the 1940s, Greenwich Village clubs offered a variety of Latin and

West Indian musicians an opportunity to perform for white and black North American audiences. Gage Averill's study of the Haitian popular band Tabou Combo reveals that the ensemble consciously marketed its sound for diverse New York and international audiences, while Wilcken's Haitian folkloric troupes often included non-Haitian performers, and played for mixed audiences.

Transplanted Caribbean musics do, of course, continue to serve as markers of in-group solidarity and pride within specific community settings. Dominicans in Washington Heights think of merengue as their music, while El Barrio's Nuyoricans identify most closely with salsa. Brooklyn's Trinidadian community trumpets its calypso and steel pan music, while the borough's Jamaican residents claim reggae as their most significant artistic achievement. But more often than not these musics serve the dual functions of defining a group's uniqueness, while creating a dialogue across ethnic boundaries and helping to negotiate relations between different cultural groups or between a minority group and the dominant culture. As Philip Kasinitz notes, Trinidadian calypso and Jamaican reggae are both components of Brooklyn's West Indian Carnival, yet each carries an island-specific connotation. Averill suggests Tabou Combo's distinctly Haitian style is purposely laced with Latin and African-American elements to appeal to Haitian and non-Haitian listeners. Paul Austerlitz notes that many New York Latin dance bands play both merengue and salsa, often for the same audience.

Austerlitz's discussion of Dominican merengue, titled "From Transplant to Transnational Circuit," underscores another critical point. Many of the best Puerto Rican, Dominican, West Indian, and Haitian musicians came to New York to take advantage of the city's sophisticated media resources that their home islands lacked. Their recordings sold to Caribbean-New Yorkers, to island audiences back home, and eventually to markets across Latin America, Europe, and Africa. New York, still home to much of the Caribbean recording industry and to large communities of transplanted migrants, remains a pivotal link in this transnational network, offering musicians, in Averill's words, a "global audience for their music." Moreover, as Averill, Austerlitz, and Peter Manuel note, within this new international arena, issues of musical taste and social identity become increasingly complex, as they must be negotiated across transethnic and transnational lines.

This collection of essays is by no means the definitive inquiry into Caribbean music in New York. None of the case studies presented here of Puerto Rican, Dominican, Trinidadian, and Haitian traditions profess to chronicle the full richness of musical activity within these respective New York communities. The contributions of musicians from Cuba and Jamaica are mentioned only in passing, while those from other smaller islands such as Barbados, the Bahamas, and Martinique are not covered at all. And perhaps most significantly, our decision to focus primarily on popular music (a category of styles that rely on mass media and commodification) led to the obvious exclusion of many domestic and sacred music practices. This emphasis accounts, as well, for the relative absence of women musicians and composers in this compilation. Women from many island cultures are only beginning to emerge from their homes and places of worship—settings in which they often lead musical activity—into the more public arena of mass marketing and mediated music. A comparative study of women's roles in the musical practices of *Santaría*, *Vodou*, and related Afro-Christian traditions in New York, could, for example, easily fill a companion volume.

Our goal is to raise issues concerning the relationship of music and social identity that will stimulate further research in New York's Caribbean communities and in other urban centers like Miami, Washington, Toronto, and London, where large numbers of island people have settled. Intensive local and comparative study of these scenes will reveal much about the nature of the diaspora process and the increasing influence of Caribbean music and culture around the world.

The editors wish to thank Carol Oja, outgoing director of the Institute for Studies in American Music, and Antonio Nadal, chair of the Caribbean Studies Program at Brooklyn College, for their assistance in planning the 1995 "Island Sounds in the Global City" conference, and their editorial advice in preparing this manuscript. Thanks also to Nancy Hager of the Conservatory of Music and Virginia Sánchez-Korrol of the Department of Puerto Rican Studies at Brooklyn College, as well as to Kathleen Krotman and Celeste Sanchez, for their conference support. Editorial suggestions from John Storm Roberts, Jeffrey Taylor, Stephen Stuempfle, Laurie Russell, John Suter, Lucia McCreery, and Michael Sumbera are greatly appreciated.

The "Island Sounds in the Global City" conference was made possible by a generous grant from the New York Council for the Humanities. Additional support for the conference and preparation of this volume came from the Recording Industries Music Performance Trust Funds, the Wolfe Institute for the Humanities at Brooklyn College, and a Brooklyn College President's Resource Grant.

NOTE

1. The most thorough survey of Caribbean music to date is Peter Manuel's *Caribbean Currents: Caribbean Music from Rumba to Reggae* (1995). See pages 72-94 and 241-243 for commentary on Latin and other Caribbean music in New York City. Other recent publications that offer useful background on Caribbean music, with occasional references to the diaspora include works by Austerlitz (1997) on Dominican merengue; Averill (1997) on Haitian popular music; Stuempfle (1995) on Trinidadian steel pan music; Guilbault (1993) on Antillean zouk; Hill (1993) on Trinidadian calypso; and Wilcken (1992) on Haitian Vodou.

REFERENCES CITED

Austerlitz, Paul. 1997. *Merengue: Dominican Music and Identity.* Philadelphia: Temple University Press.

Averill, Gage. 1997. *A Day for the Hunter, a Day for the Prey: Popular Music and Power in Haiti.* Chicago: University of Chicago Press.

Boggs, Vernon. 1992. *Salsiology: Afro-Cuban Music and the Evolution of Salsa in New York City.* New York: Excelsior Music Publishing Company.

Glasser, Ruth. 1995. *My Music Is My Flag: Puerto Rican Musicians and Their New York Communities, 1917-1940.* Berkeley: University of California Press.

Guilbault, Jocelyne. 1993. *Zouk: World Music in the West Indies.* Chicago: University of Chicago Press.

Hill, Donald. 1993. *Calypso Calaloo: Early Music in Trinidad.* Gainesville: University Press of Florida.

Manuel, Peter, with Kenneth Bilby and Michael Largey. 1995. *Caribbean Currents: Caribbean Music from Rumba to Reggae.* Philadelphia: Temple University Press.

Roberts, John Storm. 1979. *The Latin Tinge: The Impact of Latin American Music on the United States.* New York: Oxford University Press.

Stuempfle, Stephen. 1995. *The Steelband Movement: The Forging of a National Art in Trinidad and Tobago.* Philadelphia: University of Pennsylvania Press.

Sutton, Constance, and Elsa Chaney, eds. 1987. *Caribbean Life in New York City: Sociocultural Dimensions.* Staten Island, NY: The Center for Migration Studies of New York, Inc.

Wilcken, Lois. 1992. *The Drums of Vodou.* Tempe, AZ: White Cliffs Media Company.

Buscando Ambiente
Puerto Rican Musicians in New York City, 1917-1940[1]

Ruth Glasser

> People and their cultures perish in isolation, but they are born or reborn in contact with other men and women, with men and women of another culture, another creed, another race. If we do not recognize our humanity in others, we shall not recognize it in ourselves.
>
> Carlos Fuentes (1992)

On July 14, 1930, *The New York Times* reported that the country's rate of unemployment was at least twenty percent, and rising fast. On this day, eight and a half months after the stock market crash, the newspaper also showed that Prohibition had cost the United States government $960 million over the past year, in enforcement proceedings and loss of alcohol tax revenues. Just as Americans continued to drink during Prohibition, those who could afford it continued to seek amusement during the Great Depression. Singer and bandleader Cab Calloway remembered that:

> there were breadlines everywhere and near riots in New York. Everybody was angry with poor old Herbert Hoover. Everybody except people in the entertainment world, I guess. It's a funny thing, when things get really bad, when the bottom falls out of the economy, that's when people really need entertainment...Jazz was swinging, the theaters on Broadway were cleaning up, and in Harlem the nightclubs, speakeasies and jazz spots were packed every night. (Calloway and Rollins, 1976, 71).

Calloway was in a good position to know. Newly installed in Harlem's Cotton Club, he was earning about fifty thousand dollars a year. *Variety* reported that the club itself was the most profitable in New York City, netting a clear four hundred thousand dollars in its previous season.

That summer, the entertainment emanating from New York City seemed boundless. Three Rudy Vallee orchestras were playing on each Cunard Cruise ship, while the famous crooner himself had just acquired the first sponsored network radio show. Composer Cole Porter's "Love for Sale" had been banned from the airwaves for its overt references to prostitution, but many of his other songs were skyrocketing to popularity on Broadway. Vaudevillian Molly Picon was the headliner at the Palace Theater. And with a flip of the dial, highbrow New Yorkers could hear some of the first live radio broadcasts of full-scale operas.

On July 14, 1930, still another musical event was taking place in a Manhattan recording studio. While this event would never be noticed by most of the United States population, it would prove momentous to speakers of Spanish in New York and Latin America. On that day, a Puerto Rican group led by Manuel "Canario" Jiménez recorded Rafael Hernández's "Lamento Borincano." Canario and his two guitarists, *maracas* and *clave* players received about twelve dollars apiece for their efforts.

The modest fee notwithstanding, this song had a value that extended far beyond its measure in money. Just as Gorney and Harburg's "Brother, Can You Spare a Dime" (1932) became a virtual theme song for the Depression, such was "Lamento Borincano" for Puerto Ricans and other Spanish-speakers. More than any other song, this inexpensively made, apparently simple *bolero* would embody the essence of this era and the hard times it brought for many Latin Americans in both the United States and their homelands. Its basic guitar and percussion sound, its story of a peasant who goes to town to sell his crops but comes home empty-handed, brought tears to the eyes of Spanish-speakers throughout North, Central and South America.

Though it was composed and recorded in New York, "Lamento Borincano" also became a lasting, hugely popular anthem for Puerto Ricans back on the island. While the island was essentially a colony of the United States, many Puerto Ricans carved out a national identity in one of the few spheres available to them—the cultural. Songs that spoke to their experience, composed by their own compatriots—songs like "Lamento Borincano"—became emblems of this national cultural identity.

Rafael Hernández. Photo courtesy of Rafael Portela.

Despite its emotional and practical significance to *Boricuas* at home or abroad, Puerto Rican musical production remains nearly as invisible to North American audiences today as it did to their counterparts of the 1930s. Just as Puerto Rico exists in the minds of North Americans, when they think of the island at all, as a kind of netherworld, not quite Latin America, but not quite part of the United States, people in the English-speaking world have generally given little thought to the immense cultural wealth produced by Puerto Ricans. Indeed, they have had little opportunity, for while innumerable books and articles in English dissect social problems among Puerto Ricans, there are few which describe their history or artistic expressions.[2]

Puerto Ricans in general, and Puerto Rican migrants in particular, have been found more often in the pages of crisis-oriented con-

temporary studies than in those of historical works. In fact, scholars casting backward for an explanation for the persistently low
socioeconomic status of many Puerto Ricans have often blamed
this problem on an ostensible cultural deficit within the group itself. Glazer and Moynihan's 1963 contention that the Puerto Rican
heritage is "weak in folk arts, unsure in its cultural traditions, [and]
without a powerful faith" still finds its adherents thirty years later
(Glazer and Moynihan 1963, 88). Indeed, as problems multiply in
North American inner cities, there has been a recent academic and
popular revival of this blame-the-victim approach (see Chávez 1991).

Ironically, works by ethnomusicologists and music critics on Latin
popular music often reinforce this impression by taking Puerto
Rican music out of its historical context, a context that properly
includes an explanation of what happens to cultural expression
within a colonial society. Unwittingly, such writers make Puerto
Rican music the loser in an ahistorical Darwinian scheme that
closely parallels social science condemnations of Puerto Ricans as
a failed ethnic group. To them, Cuban music survived and flourished because it was the fittest. It is as if there were no political and
cultural hierarchies between colonies and neocolonies, organized
first by Spain, later by the United States. It is as if there were no
shared history to explain the similar development of musical forms
in different parts of Latin America, or the dominance of one set of
sounds over another.

The dynamics of musical production and consumption, however,
have everything to do with these political and economic colonial
structures. Bolstered by United States penetration into Latin
America, North American phonograph companies recorded largely
in Cuba and Argentina. From the early twentieth century, this was
the "Latin" music marketed throughout the world. Genres such as
the *rumba* and the *tango* enjoyed enormous popularity in large part
because of the marketing muscle of North American companies.

Since the cultural dimensions of Puerto Rican colonial and migration history remain largely unexamined, it has also become a
truism that popular Latin music in New York equals Cuban music,
even though Puerto Ricans have for many years been among the
field's most prolific performers and composers. Many popular and
scholarly assessments suggest that Puerto Rican musicians have
left their own ostensibly meager musical resources behind and
"merely" adopted Cuban sounds. Puerto Rican musicians in New
York City during the 1930s "imported" Cuban music and were
"strong in the hybridizing wing" (Manuel 1988, 46). Their own music
becomes more or less a footnote to the history of the rumba and to

subsequent popular Cuban genres. A description of the collection of contemporary Latin sounds known as *salsa*, for example, asserts that "stylistically its backbone consists of Cuban dance music" (Roberts 1979, 89).[3]

Such assertions undervalue the contributions of Puerto Rican musicians not only as laborers, but also as creators. The music and history of composers like Rafael Hernández and groups such as Canario's, for example, are fascinating in their own right, as is the interwar period when such artists wrote and played many songs of lasting beauty—within the context of the massive displacement and migration of their compatriots.

Both Rafael Hernández and Manuel "Canario" Jiménez were, in fact, part of that very working class exodus. Hernández, the son of Afro-Puerto Rican tobacco workers from the island's northwest coast, followed the pattern of many of his compatriots by migrating to San Juan and later to New York City. Like thousands of Puerto Ricans, he fought in World War One, suffering the indignities of racism as well as the honor of performing in a prestigious army band. When he came to New York, it was to work in factories, restaurants, and other menial occupations, while practicing music on the side. Many of his most famous and beautiful songs—including "Lamento Borincano"—were composed on the street corners and in the taverns of El Barrio, East Harlem.

Similarly, Canario's musical career was shaped within the context of a working-class life. A teenage stowaway who later became a merchant marine, he alternated his seafaring trade with music. When he joined Rafael Hernández's Trío Borinquen in 1925, for example, he performed between voyages. As for many musicians, Canario's economic and artistic motives were inextricably intertwined. Canario became most famous as the performer of the Afro-Puerto Rican *plena*, a coastal music he had never heard while growing up in the island's mountainous regions. When he met a group of plena musicians in New York, however, he recognized the genre's potential for popularity. Canario's prior record company connections allowed him to promote a sound with which he had little emotional connection.

Such stories show us that ethnic identity is vastly more complicated than it appears on the surface. An examination of the day-to-day experience of such music making encourages us to reevaluate the structure of ethnic history in general, and the place of ethnic cultural expression within it. Unfortunately, contemporary writings about Puerto Ricans and other ethnic North Americans, whether negative or positive, often reflect or rebel against the paradigms set up by earlier thinkers. Thus, they do not transcend previous models to consider these other possibilities.

Scholars such as Oscar Handlin, for example, writing before the 1960s, had portrayed American ethnic communities as disorganized and unhealthy settlements reflecting the abrupt uprooting of Old World, rural peoples. Their problems, he felt, were solved within a few generations through assimilation and the dissolution of the ethnic enclave (Handlin 1951). In contrast, the subsequent works of historians such as Sánchez-Korrol (1994), Yans-McLaughlin (1977), Vecoli (1964), and others have argued that these ethnic communities were highly organized environments in which family and community life reflected a coherent set of values, though not necessarily the stereotypical American ones of individualism and economic success through upward mobility. Portraits in recent ethnic monographs show music taking place in intimate gatherings within a strictly ethnically-based community setting. Their depictions of closely knit settlements, utilizing cultural activities for both ethnic and economic sustenance, constitute a reaction against earlier portrayals of immigrant cultural disorganization.

Such recent contributions have been crucial to a more three-dimensional portrait of ethnic life, especially for Puerto Ricans and other groups that have been ranked low in what Micaela di Leonardo calls "the ethnic report card system" (1984, 96). However, while such approaches bring us important new information and insights, they are also problematic. Just as Handlin praised the pastoral paradises that the immigrants had ostensibly left behind, modern historians romantically recreate such utopias in urban areas in the United States. Contemporary monographs that apparently argue against Handlin frequently follow him in presuming that "healthy" ethnic communities preserve an unspoiled and uniform Old World folk culture, exist within bounded geographical territories, and have little interaction with members of other groups. Moreover, they suggest that consensus means stability and that disagreements, divisions and change within a group of ethnic Americans indicates a community in crisis.

Evidence from both the Old World and the New World, however, suggests that such assumptions lead to serious distortions of the ethnic experience, with implications not only for the past but for contemporary societies as well. In recent years, for example, scholars have rejected simplistic rural-to-urban migration paradigms, acknowledging the variety of regional and class backgrounds from which ethnic Americans have come. Historians such as Rudolph Vecoli tell us that Italians, for example, thought of themselves as

Genoese or Calabrian back in the Old Country and only merged under one national umbrella in the United States. Such an observation would seem to be a promising beginning for a study of the subjectivity and plasticity of ethnic identity and its cultural components.

Unfortunately, while ethnic historians have begun to recognize the fragmented and constantly changing nature of the ethnic experience in economic, political and social terms, they frequently draw the same tired conclusions in the cultural realm. Historians now acknowledge the multi-faceted and ever-evolving economic, social and political reasons for immigrant and migrant movements, but persist in viewing music of the ethnics' homelands as an unmediated and uncontroversial folk sound shared by the entire community, faithfully reproduced in the United States. They do not investigate the relationship between the variety of regional, class, political, religious and other backgrounds of ethnics from the same national entity and their perceptions of national identity or their construction and use of forms of cultural expression such as music.

Historians are generally content to take both ethnicity and ethnic cultural expression as givens, as the by-products of a common national identity, the automatic offshoots of the economic and social spheres presumably underlying them. Uncritically adopting the nostalgia of their informants, for example, chroniclers of Latino music in New York City often evoke a mythically cohesive community that preserves and produces authentic music. Within such a framework, constant infusions of "genuine" music made by "real" ethnics in their own neighborhoods are ultimately diluted and commercialized by musicians catering to non-Latino audiences in the "Anglo" sections of the city. As in many other portraits of ethnic cultural life, Latinos within this framework had two choices—to remain "ethnic" (i.e. "Latin," in itself a dubious category) or to become "Americanized."[4]

Such unquestioned assumptions not only rewrite the ethnic experience within history, but impose value-laden models on contemporary ethnic life as well. These scholarly assumptions are often reflected in a popular media that tells people in the United States and other countries that they must choose between assimilation and cultural preservation. To avoid internal or external conflicts, and to be economically and socially successful, they must ally themselves with one racial or ethnic category. As a Yugoslav writer has recently pointed out, however, the culprits in interethnic strife are not multiculturalism or overlapping identities themselves but strategies of "ethnic cleansing," which are "forcing the creation of new identities that 'are so much narrower, more parochial, and less flexible'"(Denitch 1993, 21). Moreover, it is apparent that economic difficulties often provoke conflicts between peoples who previously coexisted peacefully.

Anthropologists Fredrik Barth (1969) and Micaela di Leonardo (1984), historian David Whisnant (1983), ethnomusicologist Adelaida Reyes-Schramm (1975), and sociologist Felix Padilla (1985) suggest, however, that rather than indicating the deterioration of a community and its cultural practices, the constant evolutions of ethnic identity and spheres such as music are normal historical processes. Within any living society, ongoing intra- and inter-ethnic negotiation and reshaping of cultural forms in dialogue with material conditions are the stuff of which national and ethnic identities are made and remade. Indeed, I concur with Eric Hobsbawm and Terence Ranger's contention that tradition itself often amounts to a set of conventions from a variety of sources, agreed upon by a self-defined group of people, that are frequently redefined in moments of rapid social transformation (Hobsbawm and Ranger 1983).

Puerto Ricans on the island and the mainland did not adopt Cuban music wholesale to the detriment of their own traditions, but incorporated it into an ever-evolving repertoire of available cultural materials. In New York, where Puerto Ricans lived among a constellation of constantly changing ethnic groups within a protean social environment, this process accelerated and perhaps became more acutely meaningful. The diverse collection of Puerto Rican migrants who found themselves living, sometimes together and sometimes apart, in New York City did not unite behind a common ethnic identity represented by agreed-upon institutions and cultural symbols. Instead, they formed a range of organizations and debated over appropriate cultural programs and representative repertoires. They exchanged forms of entertainment and ideas about its purpose among themselves as well as with members of other ethnic groups.

Puerto Rican communities in New York were neither ethnically inviolable nor disintegrating, and their cultural choices were far broader than an "ethnic" or an "American" identity. The musical trajectories of many Puerto Rican performers bear this out. Rafael Hernández's groups played and recorded Cuban *habaneras*, Colombian *bambucos* and a host of other Latin American genres. Others worked for recording studios as session musicians, playing behind a spectrum of ethnic groups.

Sometimes such trajectories were more a matter of constraint than of choice. Afro-Puerto Rican musicians such as Augusto Coen, for example, found their careers limited by the racism of the North American entertainment industry. Like many black Puerto Ricans, this Ponce-born trumpeter was barred from work with the lighter-skinned Latino "relief" bands, groups that played between white American orchestras at elegant midtown clubs and hotels. Unlike their lighter-skinned compatriots, Afro-Puerto Rican musicians could not play with the popular white swing bands of the era.

On the other hand, such constraints funnelled Coen and his colleagues into new creative channels and musical combinations. As reading musicians who were well-trained in Puerto Rico's municipal bands, these Afro-Puerto Ricans were eagerly grabbed for black

Augusto Coen (front, standing with baton) and his Golden Casino Orchestra. Photo courtesy of the Centro de Estudios Puertorriqueños, Hunter College, CUNY.

shows on Broadway and by some of the finest African-American ensembles of the day. Coen himself had opportunities to play with Duke Ellington, Noble Sissle, and Fletcher Henderson. After spending a few years in the band of Afro-Cuban flutist Alberto Socarrás, Coen formed his own group, Augusto Coen y Sus Boricuas. The bands of Socarrás and Coen drew upon their members' apprenticeships with African-American ensembles, becoming possibly the first groups in New York to combine jazz and Latin music.

Whether through choice or constraint, musical subcultures often exist side by side or within a dominant culture, with varying

degrees of exchange and mutual influence. Examples of the complex dynamics inherent in such diffuse expression quickly emerge
when one scrutinizes musical production and its social, political
and economic context.[5] North Americans between the World Wars
were usually oblivious to the rich Spanish-language musical production going on in their own country—unless it was danceable.
Most Puerto Ricans, however, were conversant in the popular mainstream styles and artists of the period, and even used them as a
point of reference for their own. A 1930 ad in New York's major
Spanish newspaper, *La Prensa*, for example, billed the popular Cuban singer Antonio Machín as "el Rudy Vallee cubano," that is, the
Cuban Rudy Vallee.[6] Clearly, imbalanced power relations between
groups and countries can have subtle cultural correlatives although
musical expression is not reducible only to this interpretation.

Music is a compelling subject of study precisely because it is simultaneously a material and symbolic phenomenon. As Raymond
Williams and William Roseberry suggest, "cultural objects are embedded in a process of creation and reception such that cultural
creation is itself a form of material production, [so] that the ab-
stract distinction between material base and ideal superstructure
dissolves in the face of a material social process through which
both 'material' and 'ideal' are constantly created and recreated"
(Roseberry 1989, 26). Songs such as "Lamento Borincano" or, for
that matter, "Love for Sale," are, concretely speaking, the mediated
products of the entertainment industry. Musicians are workers producing tangible products, and music itself often follows trade routes
and is made up of concrete mixes that we can trace. A musical analysis of "Lamento Borincano," for example, would show the influences of Italian opera, Puerto Rican mountain music, and Cuban
popular sounds.

And yet music is not reducible to its commercial and genealogi-
cal dimensions. By musicological standards, there was nothing particularly Puerto Rican or folkloric about "Lamento Borincano."
Nevertheless, many Puerto Ricans immortalized it as a profound
expression of national consciousness. The symbolic importance of
this song forces us to re-examine the causal relationship between
music and the social, political and economic conditions intersect-
ing with it. Although musical production is dependent upon the
conditions of what I hesitatingly call this larger setting, it also pos-
sesses its own internal dynamics. The lives of musicians are simultaneously based in economics and aesthetics, and their production
is both symbolic and concrete. They span both sides of this traditional causal divide and thus provide a significant case study with
which we can re-evaluate our preconceptions of what produces what.

In many cases, musical forms actually serve to articulate and even define social distinctions, a point nicely illustrated in Manuel Peña's (1985) study of music among Mexican-Americans in Texas. At the same time, music is unpredictable and can often transcend social, economic and political conditions and class, racial, ethnic and geographic barriers that its audiences cannot.

There are many ways in which Puerto Rican music, or indeed any ethnic music, both relates to other spheres and yet creates its own. For example, while tens of thousands of Puerto Ricans settled in New York prior to World War Two, this migration in no way equaled the one following the war. And yet it was precisely this period between the world wars that produced the most fervently patriotic Puerto Rican music by the most beloved Puerto Rican popular composers of this century. Moreover, many of these songs, such as Hernández's "Lamento Borincano" and Pedro Flores' "Sin Bandera," were composed in New York City.

There were ironies in such music's relationship to other ethnic sounds, which seemed mainstream by comparison. During economically desperate times, as we have seen, Cab Calloway was earning one thousand dollars a week. But Calloway's theory regarding the direct relationship between hard times and entertainment is foiled when one remembers that Canario and many other artists were probably earning thirty dollars or less in the same week that Calloway pocketed his thousand. In any given time, as well as over time, ethnic musical production is multi-layered and subject to a range of influences. The songs made by Rafael Hernández, for example, were as embedded as those of Cole Porter in the recording and publishing industries' organization of production and distribution, and yet they were marketed to vastly different audiences and yielded very disparate rewards to their composers.

The way Puerto Ricans made meaning of their music and musicians, and how they decided what was an authentic or traditional expression, varied between social groups as well as individuals, always in a dialectic with the concrete conditions under which the music was produced. Music in Puerto Rico was subject to foreign and commercial influences as well as differences in race, class, and regional development, and in New York it continued to be protean, shaped according to situation and evolving through time. Rather than serving as a unifying force in a dividing or dissolving United States ethnic community, music itself was an ongoing source of diverse definitions for Puerto Rican ethnic identity and an arena of contention. Just as the music they created and were exposed to was complex and mediated, so were the responses to it of people with varying and ever-evolving ideas about their cultural identity. On

the island blacks and whites, upper and lower classes danced to the
same mixes of Spanish, Cuban, Puerto Rican, European and North
American ballroom music—in separate clubs. As expatriates in New
York, some Boricuas celebrated their Latino identity and the wealth
of musical forms it embraced. Other Puerto Ricans, both working
class and elite, complained of the lack of a truly "pure" national
music.

During the early decades of the twentieth century, both Puerto
Rico and New York witnessed disputes and disagreements among
ethnic musicians, audiences and industry personnel as to what was
authentic Puerto Rican music and what ought to be recorded and
played at live events. The plena, for example, was rejected by white
elites in Puerto Rico because of its black proletarian origins, African percussion, and satirical lyrics. But when Canario adopted and
recorded the plena in New York, the genre began to gain more widespread acceptance. The presence of Canario and other light-skinned
musicians and the group's use of more melodic and fewer percussion instruments changed many Puerto Ricans' perceptions of the
music. At a safe distance from Puerto Rico, the satirical lyrics were
no longer as biting and topical. Nostalgic and lost among a sea of
other ethnic groups, New York's Puerto Ricans were also eager to
adopt forms of music they could call their own.

Such histories show that the ethnic cultural experience is often a
highly subjective and plastic one, within which ethnic peoples indi-
vidually mold their collective identities, drawing from a broad repertoire of cultural forms.[7] This experience draws upon the ongoing
contact between the old country and the new, a phenomenon that
historians often overlook. It is particularly vital, of course, in the
case of Puerto Ricans, for political, economic, and geographical
reasons.

Puerto Rican music, like any living cultural form, was always
subject to a mix of influences on the island as well as in New York
City. North American and Puerto Rican musicians, for example,
have for a long time been aware of the existence of each others'
music, and neither they nor their audiences have been as reluctant
to accept its hybridization as ethnic histories generally lead us to
believe.

Just as Puerto Rican music between the world wars was diverse,
a large collection of different people helped to bring it into concrete
form. These included composers, performers, audiences, local merchants and clubowners, record company executives, and that most
elusive of all figures, the ethnic intermediary, an individual who
served as a cultural broker between Puerto Rican musicians and

the New York music industry. As Howard S. Becker and other sociologists of cultural production would put it, art is a social activity and "whether we speak of the collective acts of a few people...or those of a much larger number...we always need to ask who is acting together to create what events" (Becker 1982).

This team of players, however, did not perform on a level playing field. Many of the forces producing such new and diverse combinations of music, including economic pressures upon musicians and a North American near monopoly on the production of commercial entertainment, have been anything but benign or in the hands of Puerto Ricans. In pre-World War Two New York (and for that matter, up to the present) Puerto Ricans worked within a music business they did not control. At the same time, musicians and audiences made choices that reflected their own intertwined economic and aesthetic motives and musical and social relationships. Puerto Rican composers and performers crafted their own words to these "foreign" musical genres and prided themselves on their ability to please a wide variety of dancers and listeners. Likewise, audiences were proud of their musical compatriots who were successful in their careers. Rather than feeling a sense of anger and ethnic betrayal when Puerto Rican musicians began to play with the Catalan Xavier Cugat or the North American Paul Whiteman, their compatriots, who generally lived in the same neighborhoods and worked in the same daytime jobs, felt that these musicians were bringing credit to Puerto Ricans as a whole, as well as money and new sounds into the community. Canario's musicians did not despise him because he adopted the style and songs of others and was not as talented as they were. They were glad his hustling abilities brought them work.

Musical production had its own nuances in the more technical spheres. Influenced by economic downturns or international problems that cut off supplies of materials and artists, record production was also tremendously affected by changes within the medium itself. Ethnic recording had its own particularities. During the Depression, for example, when other types of record sales plummeted, Spanish-language discs stayed steady and even flourished. Never a dramatic sales area for companies even in the best of times, ethnic records continued to do what they had always done: they provided a means for manufacturers to sell phonographs to homesick United States migrants and immigrants. The rise of radio, which drastically affected mainstream record sales from the mid-1920s, had little effect on those ethnic groups toward whom few programs were geared at that time.

The history of Puerto Rican music in New York City is thus a history of infinite crossovers and variations on a theme. It is a history that reflects the conditions surrounding it and yet escapes them. Puerto Ricans have defied scholars' long-standing categories by popularizing folk music and folklorizing popular music. In-depth study of this music within its social and historical context is both enriching in its own right and has a lot to teach us about the dynamics of ethnic musical production in general.

NOTES

1. Portions of this article are adapted from Ruth Glasser's "Introduction: Buscando Ambiente," *My Music Is My Flag: Puerto Rican Musicians and Their New York Communities, 1917-1940* (1995, 1-12).

2. A notable work, and still sadly enough, the exception, is Virginia Sánchez-Korrol's *From Colonia to Community: The History of Puerto Ricans in New York City* (1994).

3. This is not to suggest that the overall history of Cuban popular music has been adequately covered, especially in English. Aside from brief references to the *rumba* era of the 1930s, chronicles of Cuban music in New York usually focus on its development from the 1940s to the present. Nevertheless, enthusiasts of Cuban music have at least some resources to turn to.

4. See, for example, Roberts (1979), Salazar (1981), and Leymarie (1994).

5. Mark Slobin and Richard Spottswood (1985), for example, analyze the eclectic career of an early twentieth century Jewish musician, noting his not atypical "inter-ethnic popular culture contact" and "fluency in two parallel, related, yet complementary ethnic styles."

6. Advertisement, *La Prensa* (New York City), 13 June 1930.

7. di Leonardo's *The Varieties of Ethnic Experience* (1984), particularly Chapters Four and Five, have been instrumental in helping me to draw such conclusions based on my own research in New York and Puerto Rico. So has my multi-ethnic musical research and organizing in Waterbury, Connecticut, shared and interpreted with Jeremy Brecher.

REFERENCES CITED

Barth, Fredrik, ed. 1969. *Ethnic Groups and Boundaries*. Boston: Little, Brown.

Becker, Howard S. 1982. *Art Worlds*. Berkeley: University of California Press.

Calloway, Cab, and Brian Rollins. 1976. *Of Minnie the Moocher and Me*. New York: Thomas Y. Crowell Co.

Chávez, Linda. 1991. *Out of the Barrio: Towards a New Politics of Hispanic Assimilation*. New York: Basic Books.

Denitch, Bogdan. Quoted in Jeremy Brecher, John Brown Childs and Jill Cutler, eds. 1993. *Global Visions: Beyond the New World Order*. Boston: South End Press.

di Leonardo, Micaela. 1984. *The Varieties of Ethnic Experience: Kinship, Class and Gender Among California Italian-Americans*. Ithaca: Cornell University Press.

Fuentes, Carlos. 1992. "Hispanic U.S.A.: A Mirror of the Other." *The Nation* 411, no. 12 (March): 254.

Glasser, Ruth. 1995. *My Music Is My Flag: Puerto Rican Musicians and Their New York Communities, 1917-1940*. Berkeley: University of California Press.

Glazer, Nathan, and Daniel Moynihan. 1963. *Beyond the Melting Pot: The Negroes, Puerto Ricans, Jews, Italians and Irish of New York City*. Cambridge: M.I.T. Press.

Handlin, Oscar. 1951. *The Uprooted*. New York: Grosset and Dunlap.

Hobsbawm, Eric, and Terence Ranger, eds. 1983. *The Invention of Tradition*. New York: Cambridge University Press.

Leymarie, Isabelle. 1994. "Salsa and Migration." In *The Commuter Nation*, ed. William Burgos, Carlos Torre and Hugo Vecchini. Rio Piedras: University of Puerto Rico Press.

Manuel, Peter. 1988. *Popular Musics of the Non-Western World*. New York: Oxford University Press.

Padilla, Felix. 1985. *Latino Ethnic Consciousness*. Notre Dame: University of Notre Dame Press.

Peña, Manuel. 1985. *The Texas-Mexican Conjunto: History of a Working-Class Music*. Austin: University of Texas Press.

Reyes-Schramm, Adelaida. 1975. "The Role of Music in the Interaction of Black Americans and Hispanics in New York City's East Harlem." Ph.D. diss., Columbia University.

Roberts, John Storm. 1979. *The Latin Tinge: The Impact of Latin American Music on the United States*. New York: Oxford University Press.

Roseberry, William. 1989. *Anthropologies and Histories*. New Brunswick: Rutgers University Press.

Salazar, Max. 1981. "History of Afro-Cuban Music." *Sonido* 1:1.

Sánchez-Korrol, Virginia. 1994. *From Colonia to Community: The History of Puerto Ricans in New York City*. Berkeley: University of California Press.

Slobin, Mark, and Richard Spottswood. 1985. "David Medoff: A Case Study in Inter-Ethnic Popular Culture." *American Music* 3(3) (Fall): 261, 263.

Vecoli, Rudolph. 1964. "Contadini in Chicago: A Critique of the Uprooted." *Journal of American History* (December): 404-417.

Whisnant, David. 1983. *All That is Native and Fine: The Politics of Culture in an American Region*. Chapel Hill: University of North Carolina Press.

Yans-McLaughlin, Virginia. 1977. *Family and Community: Italian Immigrants in Buffalo, 1880-1930*. Ithaca: Cornell University Press.

Representations of New York City in Latin Music

Peter Manuel

Urban migrant cultures are now recognized as dynamic, syncretic entities in their own right, rather than derivative, transplanted outposts, miniature replicas of ancestral homeland models, or inherently marginal hybrids. New York City's Latino society is exemplary in this respect; Latin New York, once an isolated enclave, has become the single most important center of urban Spanish-Caribbean culture and of Latin music as well. Meanwhile, the ancestral homelands themselves have in many respects become cultural, economic, and political satellites of the United States and especially of New York. This process has involved demographic factors (the emergence of a critical mass of New York Latinos in the 1960s), economic ones (the dominance of North American capital), and—of greatest interest here—cultural ones, including a new sense of ethnic and socio-geographic identity among New York Latinos.

In recent decades, our understanding of Latin New York has been immeasurably aided by scholarly studies, from the ethnographies of Oscar Lewis (1968) and Ruth Glasser (1995) to the theoretical insights of Juan Flores (1991; 1994). This essay will illustrate how song texts, from the earliest period of migration to the present, constitute emic documents articulating the growth of New York Latin culture, both in its broad stages and in many aspects of its affective nuances. Of course, one must exercise caution in trying to "read off" cultural history and social reality from song lyrics. Word-oriented folkloric genres like Puerto Rican *jíbaro* music, which constituted a rich oral literature, have declined in recent decades, and in dance musics like *salsa* and modern *merengue*, song texts are relatively unimportant elements. Moreover, only a minority of

Latin music song texts produced by the New York community speak explicitly of the urban experience. Finally, the song lyrics that do become accessible beyond the immediate local community (including to relative outsiders like myself) are those that have been mediated and conditioned by the commercial entertainment industry, which exercises its own idiosyncratic influences and pressures.

Nevertheless, a substantial number of song texts do address the New York experience. If they constitute only a minority, it is a significant minority, and their content can be seen to reveal much about popular attitudes and experiences. Moreover, while driving rhythms and brilliant arrangements are of greater importance than lyrics in dance music, many song texts do become memorable, long-cherished, and uniquely influential classics of Latin culture, the most celebrated examples being songs of Rubén Blades like "Pedro Navaja." Crooners in the shower sing lyrics rather than bass lines, and songs are recalled and indicated by evocative, text-derived titles rather than technical criteria (with prosaic exceptions like Pérez Prado's "Mambo #8" proving the rule). Hence, song texts, with certain qualifications, can indeed be taken as significant and heuristic expressions of lived social reality.

Latino scholars and journalists have commented on several features of contemporary song lyrics, and aspects of the New York presence—especially ghetto life and Nuyorican identity—have been tangentially discussed by a few writers, especially César Rondón in his magisterial *El libro de la salsa* (1980). Here I will focus on the ways that song texts over the decades portray a changing conception of New York in relation to other locations in the sociomusical landscape of the Caribbean Basin. Lyric depictions of New York can be seen to represent stages, viewing the city initially as a lonely outpost, then as a troubled homeland and cultural epicenter, and lastly, in a more subtle fashion, as one of several lodestars in an increasingly diverse, international, and postmodern musical soundscape.

"Island in the City"
New York as an Immigrant Outpost

The Latino community that developed in New York from the turn of the century was overwhelmingly Puerto Rican until the late 1970s, when massive Dominican immigration changed the subculture's complexion. Accordingly, as Ruth Glasser (1995) and others have shown, by the 1920s New York had come to play a significant role in the evolution of Puerto Rican music, due in part to the presence of the recording industry, the acute sense of ethnic self-consciousness felt by migrants as being simultaneously painful and creatively stimulating (see Flores 1991, 16), and the presence of leading artists, especially composers Rafael Hernández and Pedro Flores, and *bolero* and *plena* singer Manuel "Canario" Jiménez.

The commercial recordings of Puerto Rican music that became widespread from the 1920s were mostly produced in New York, whose small but concentrated barrio communities constituted natural markets. As the Nuyorican population grew exponentially from the 1940s, more and more songs dealt directly or indirectly with the experience of migration. Although historically remote, the music of this period is relatively rich in chronicling urban life, since text-oriented folk genres like jíbaro (*campesino*) music and traditional plena (a topical, mostly urban syncretic folksong genre) were still flourishing, and most recordings were conducted in New York rather than on the island (Glasser 1995, 50).

The most salient feature of these songs' lyrics is their documentation of an initial stage—the migrant stage—in which New York is clearly an outpost, while the island (in this period, Puerto Rico) remains the spiritual and psychological home. In the early decades of the record industry, one indication of this orientation was that the vast majority of songs recorded in New York dealt with island rather than mainland life (Spottswood and Díaz Ayala 1989), whether out of habit or a sense that New York was a soulless place about which little could be sung. Such songs included Hernández's classic hymn to the impoverished homeland, "Lamento Borincano," written in New York in 1929 (see Glasser 1995, 163ff), portraying the decline of jíbaro life and of the island's fortunes in general. From the late 1920s, however, boleros, plenas, and jíbaro songs (*seis, aguinaldo*) started to address life in the Yankee metropolis. Nevertheless, most of these songs remained oriented toward the island in one way or another, just as Puerto Rican music in New York remained at this point essentially a transplanted island music.

In the 1940s, the New York-based *mambo* bands of Machito and Antonio Arcaño were invoking the city's glamour and excitement in titles like "Mambo a la Savoy" and "Conozca a New York" ("Get to Know New York"). For most migrants, however, the quotidian reality of urban life was far from glamorous. As dispossessed peasants poured into New York, they developed an entire subgenre of jíbaro songs that chronicled the vicissitudes of life in the metropolis. Their songs speak, often with poignant humor, of brutal winters, of getting lost for days in the subway, or of the difficulties encountered from not speaking English:

Yo vine por Nueva York
porque yo me imaginaba
que aquí se hablaba
el Inglés aligual que el Español
pero me dijo un señor
"no, tú estás muy equivocado
cuando quiere bacalao
tiene que decir co'fi'"...
en qué apuros me veo
cuando llego al restaurant
al decirme "Wha' you wan'?"
les señalo con el dedo.

———————

I came to New York because I thought
that they spoke as much Spanish as English;
but here they told me
"No you're quite mistaken
When you want *bacalao*
you have to say co'fi'"[codfish]...
I feel so ridiculous in the restaurant
when they ask "Wha' you wan'?"
and I have to point with my finger.[1]

Other songs—especially sentimental boleros—conflate nostalgia for the *patria* with longing for a beloved left behind, as in Pedro Flores' classic "Bajo un palmar." Several aguinaldos depict the yearning for distant relatives, which became particularly acute at Christmas season, when family gatherings (often with aguinaldo singing) are customary.

Some songs portray the adversity of New York life as unbearable, such that the narrator laments selling his plot of land in order to migrate. In Ramito's "Yo me quedo en Puerto Rico," the singer resolves to return to Puerto Rico, even if it means dying in poverty:

¿Quién fue el que me dijo a mí
que me fuera a Nueva Yor'?
el ambiente era mejor
y diferente de aquí
pero yo que he estado allí
si hay que criticar critico
allí solo se ve un pico
el del Empire Sta'

Yo no dejo mi batey
y yo me quedo en Puerto Rico.

Yo me fuí por tiempo breve
para el tiempo de invierno
vivir allí es un infierno
atropella'o con la nieve
¿Quién a decirme se atreve
que deje el terruño chico
y abandone el abanico
del astro sol borinqueño?
Vivir allá no es mi empeño
y yo me quedo en Puerto Rico.

Dios guarde me Borikén
llena de amor y de alegría
donde se da la yautía
el yame y el panapén
Vivir aquí es un Eden
eso yo lo justifico
aquí a nadie perjudico
Me como lo que me sobre
No me importa que muera pobre
si yo me quedo en Puerto Rico.

Who was it who told me to go to New York,
that it was better there, and different from here?
Now that I've been there,
if there are things to criticize then I'll say so.
All you see is the peak of the Empire State Building.
I won't give up my sugar mill, I'm staying in Puerto Rico.

I went for a short visit, during winter.
It's hell living there, tramping around in the snow.
Who would dare tell me that I should give up my little
plot of land and abandon my hand fan
of the Puerto Rican lodestar?
Living there is not for me, I'm staying in Puerto Rico.

God protect my Borinquén full of love and happiness
where you can get *yautía, yame* and *panapen* [local foods].
It is like living in a Garden of Eden here.
I tell you, I don't harm a soul here,

I eat whatever food is left over.
I don't care if I die poor, if I stay in Puerto Rico.[2]

Another classic articulation of the same sentiment is "Yo Vuelvo
a mi Bohío," "I'm Going Back to my Shack," by El Jibarito de
Adjuntas (ca. 1951):

Si yo vine a Nueva York
con el fin de progresar
si allá lo pasaba mal
aquí lo paso peor
Unas veces el calor
y otras el maldito frío
a veces parezco un lío
por la nieve patinando
eso no me está gustando
yo me vuelvo a mi bohío

I came to New York hoping to get ahead,
But if it was bad back home, here it's worse.
Sometimes it's hot, and other times freezing cold.
Sometimes I look like a bundle sliding around on the snow.
I don't like this, I'm going back to my hut.[3]

In such songs, the portrayal of New York is unambiguously negative, as a cold and harsh outpost to which migrants are driven by
poverty. Puerto Rico, although impoverished, remains the warm,
lush, spiritually endowed *patria*, the *cristalino manantial* (pure
mountain spring),[4] the site of the heart and soul, of the beloved, the
family, and the traditional culture that provides meaning, coher-
ence, and beauty to life. Thus, while Rafael Hernández's "Pura
Flama" depicts the narrator sampling New York women of various
ethnicities, it is only in Puerto Rico that he can find love (see Glasser
1995, 145-46). While not mentioning New York, the innumerable
patriotic boleros and jíbaro songs of this period that eulogize Puerto
Rico's beauty can be seen as counterpoints to the barrio chronicles,
implicitly celebrating the island as an antipode possessing everything that New York lacks. At the same time, the songs dealing with
migrant life conflate with another island song category, namely, the
many nostalgic songs (such as "Lamento Borincano") romanticizing the pre-modern, pre-capitalist, rural past, and lamenting the
alienation and impersonality of modernity and the decline of jíbaro
life.[5] Similarly, a jíbaro song like Chuito's 1974 "La Mujer en Nueva

York" ("The Woman in New York"), bewailing the alleged moral decline of migrant women, reflects a broader Latin American and Caribbean male discourse about the negative effects of urbanization on women. This discourse would include not only certain Dominican *bachatas* (see Pacini Hernández 1995, 164), but also colonial-era calypsos like Tiger's 1937 "Maraval Girls" and literary works like René Marqués' play *La Carreta*, which dramatizes the moral and economic ruin of a Puerto Rican migrant family (see Aparicio i.p., ch. 8).

New York: The Troubled Homeland

In other songs dealing with life in New York, the narrator portrays a more positive and pragmatic attitude. Such songs can be seen as representing a second stage of the New York Latino experience, in which the migrants adjust to city life and begin to gradually detach themselves emotionally from the island homeland. In his 1936 plena "¡Qué vivío!" ("What a way of life!"), Canario (Manuel Jiménez) celebrates his ability to live off welfare in the city:

> No me voy, no me voy, no me voy de Nueva York
> Aquí me pagan la casa, me dan ternera con papa
> y carne de lata, que es un primor.

> I won't leave, I won't leave, I won't leave New York.
> Here they pay my rent and give me veal and potato
> and canned meat, which is terrific.[6]

In a similar vein, Ismael Santiago's 1967 plena, "La Metrópolis," relates:

> En esta metrópolis se critica la vida
> pero si nos vamos volvemos en seguida...
> soy puertorriqueño y quiero mi islita
> pero yo no critico donde gano la vida
> ya no me arrepiento el traer a mi familia
> porque mi barrio es mi segunda islita
> como cuchifritos aguacates y china
> y una borinqueña es mi mejor vecina

> People criticize life in this city,
> But if they leave, they come back right away...
> I'm Puerto Rican and I love my island

but I don't criticize where I earn my living.
I don't regret bringing my family here anymore
because my barrio is my second little island.
Here I eat *cuchifritos*, avocados and oranges
and a Puerto Rican woman is my best neighbor [7]

A 1929 plena, "En la 116" ("On 116th St."), depicts the narrator
enjoying the movies, learning some English, and having a Puerto
Rican sweetheart next door.[8] However, even if these songs portray
their protagonists adjusting to life in their new surroundings, many
of them retain a clear orientation toward the island. "¡Qué Vivío!"
and "La Metrópolis" are unpretentiously worldly in their practical
and material rationalizations for staying in New York, which, in
the latter song, is identified not as home, but merely a place where
the singer earns his living. What makes New York tolerable is not
its intrinsic qualities, but the ways in which it is a miniature Puerto
Rico—"my second little island"—with Puerto Rican foods and neighbors. Meanwhile, "En la 116" concludes by relating how regional
island loyalties continue to condition migrant life:

Pues yo como soy de Ponce y ella es de Mayagüe'
su madre a mí no me habla, pues con su hijo yo me casé.

Because I'm from Ponce and she's from Mayagüez
her mother won't talk to me, since I married her daughter.

Since the late 1960s, songs about the Puerto Rican migration
experience have become less numerous and significant. Islanders
have continued to migrate, but what has become more common is
what Juan Flores has described as a circulatory process in which
Puerto Ricans travel back and forth on the "air bus" ("*La guagua
aérea*," in the words of Luis Rafael Sánchez) over the "blue pond" of
the Atlantic (Flores 1991, 17). While monolingual islanders still have
difficulty in Anglophone New York, equally common is the phenomenon of Nuyoricans or long-time migrants having forgotten their
Spanish—willfully, in some cases—as whimsically dramatized in
Sonora Ponceña's "Un jíbaro en Nueva York":

Me refiero a los hispano'
que lleganse [unclear] a Nueva Yo'
y al tirarse del avión
se le olvida el castellano

ayer me encontré a Mariano
un jíbaro de Jagüey
que al montarse en el subway
le pregunté como estaba
"I don' know wha' you say"

I'm talking about the Latinos
who come to New York
and as soon as they get off the plane
they forget their Spanish.
Yesterday I ran into Mariano
a jíbaro from Jagüey
getting on the subway.
When I asked him how he was
he answered,
"I don't know what you say."[9]

Meanwhile, as the island itself has become more modernized and Americanized, migration to the mainland has become less traumatic and jarring.

The Dominican Invasion

While Puerto Rican migration has declined in numbers and importance, it has been succeeded by a massive wave of immigrants (legal and otherwise) from the Dominican Republic. Driven by ambition, poverty, political repression, and fascination with the *"gran manzana,"* roughly a half million Dominicans have settled in New York since the latter 1970s, revitalizing upper Manhattan's Washington Heights ("Quisqueya Heights") and altering the character of the city's Latino population. In the process, the Dominican merengue brought by the newcomers has become widely popular among Nuyoricans and even in Puerto Rico itself.

Several Dominican merengues address the migration experience, often in terms quite similar to earlier Puerto Rican songs. Some merengue texts chronicle the hardships of New York barrio life, with its pervasive crime, drugs, and impersonality. In "Nueva York es Así" ("That's How New York Is"), La Patrulla 15 sings:

Papá quiero irme a Nueva York para vivir un chipito mejor
porque con este jornal no puedo sacar a mi novia a bailar.

Father, I want to go to New York to live a bit better

because on this salary I can't even take my girlfriend out
dancing.

After borrowing some verses from a 1950s bolero ("Sin un Amor"),
the singer goes on to describe the crime, the cold, the inaccessibil-
ity of the city's beautiful women, the temptation to break the law
and the consequences of doing so, and the constant danger (for
illegal immigrants) of being apprehended and deported. The chorus warns:

> Nueva York no es así, no es como me imagina
> quédate en tu país que ahí sí es verdad que hay vida.
> ———————
> New York isn't like this, not like I imagined.
> Stay in your own country,
> because it's true that there's a life there.[10]

In a more positive vein, such songs as Ramon Orlando's "Nueva
York No Duerme" ("New York Doesn't Sleep") extol the city's dyna-
mism and excitement. Others present New York as a land of opportunity, from which the enterprising migrant can return *para'o*—
in style, well-heeled, well-prepared.

> Todos e felicitaron cuando vino del lado
> vino con siete maletas...
> para'o, el hombre llegó para'o, para'o, para'o...
> ———————
> Everyone congratulated him when he came
> from the other side.
> He came with seven suitcases, he arrived in style.[11]

By the mid-1990s, New York has become the first home to so
many Dominicans that its vicissitudes, rewards, and fast pace—at
once hectic and exhilarating—can be described in a matter-of-fact
way, as in the song "Un Día en Nueva York" by Los Hermanos
Rosario. The lyrics to this song begin with a by-now familiar lament:

> Para yo [*sic*] vivir aquí no ha sido fácil
> en un apartment en pleno Bronx
> si no es un tiroteo, la sirena
> cuando no es una ganga, es un "hold-up."
> ———————

It hasn't been easy living here
in an apartment in the middle of the Bronx.
If it's not gunfire outside, it's a siren,
or if it's not a gang, it's a hold-up.[12]

In characteristic merengue style, however, the subsequent lyrics are light and glib rather than poignant, describing the narrator's busy and stimulating daily routine, and punctuated by the refrain "¡Qué vacilón!"—loosely, "What a party!"

A few merengues, like earlier jíbaro songs, focus on the fate of the displaced campesino—here, the rustic bumpkin from Cibao Valley—in the urban jungle. Wilfrido Vargas' "El Gringo y el Cibaeño" is representative, facetiously portraying an argument between a condescending Yankee and a fiercely patriotic Dominican who loves his cassava and *chicharrones* (fried pork rinds):

Un cibaeño en Nueva York discutía con emoción
con un trompetista gringo la razón
de su desvelo por su tierra y su región
El gringo nunca se entendía cómo aquel dominicano
querría dejar a Manhattan para regresar a su tierra,
San José de las Matas
Defendía a Nueva York aquel gringo colorado
y oiga que el dominicano defendiendo su Cibao
(Gringo:) yo vivo en Santo Domingo, pero déme la razón,
no compare tu país, ni siquiera con el Bronx,
jamás con el Bronx
(Cibaeño:) No me ponga ningun Bronx de punta
comparición te lo cambio por el casave...
(G:) *Very upset* mi buen señor usted debe comprender,
que en tu pueblo no ha soña'o un Empire State
nunca no ha soñao tener un Empire State
(C:) ¿Qué me importa el Empire State?
No vaya creer que es demasiado,
Te voy a cambiar en el menomento [monumento]
que hay en la entrada de Santiago
(G:) ¡Viva la Quinta Avenida, viva Rockefeller Center!
si te monta' en el subway vera'gozar a la gente
...right here, siento aquí happy, I feel really good,
cruisin' in the street, with my favorite girl,
riding through the park, through Central Park...
(C:) Que en Nueva York no se goza mucho,

no hombre no embrome usted allá se goza bailando merengue con mi copa de cherche...

A Cibaeño in New York was arguing
with a gringo trumpet player,
about the Cibaeño's concern for his country and his region.
The gringo couldn't understand why the Dominican
wanted to leave Manhattan to return to his home,
San José de las Matas.
The pink-skinned gringo defended New York,
while the Dominican defended his Cibao.
(Gringo:) I live in Santo Domingo, tell me now
don't compare your country with mine,
not even with the Bronx, never with the Bronx.
(Cibaeño:) Don't talk to me about the Bronx,
I'd rather have some cassava.
(G:) [I'm] very upset, my good sir, you must understand.
In your village they've never even dreamed
of having an Empire State Building,
never even dreamed of it there.
(C:) What do I care about the Empire State Building?
Don't think it's so special.
I'll trade it for the monument in the entrance to Santiago.
(G:) Long live Fifth Avenue! Long live Rockefeller Center!
If you go on the subway you'll see people enjoying
themselves...right here, I feel happy, I feel really good,
cruisin' in the street, with my favorite girl,
riding through the park, through Central Park...
(C:) In New York you can't really have fun,
don't kid yourself.
[In Santo Domingo] you can have fun dancing merengue,
drinking *cherche*... [13]

Such lyrics continue the tradition of songs about the New York
experience from the perspective of the Spanish-Caribbean immigrant, although with somewhat distinctive nuances. For one thing,
the typical Dominican musical vehicle is the manic and ironic merengue, rather than the wistful bolero or poignant aguinaldo. Further, in these songs, as in the realm of Dominican music as a whole,
there is little romanticization of the idyllic homeland; rather, the
lack of sentimentality accords with the traditionally weak sense of
Dominican nationalism (Black 1986, 7), and also, to some extent,
with the prevailing pragmatism and light cynicism of the present
era—a topic to which I will return.

Salsa: the Voice of the Barrio

With the emergence of salsa in the mid-1960s, depictions of the New York experience enter a qualitatively new stage. In the salsa of this period, the barrio is the new center of gravity, and the ancestral homeland is remote, imaginary, and in many respects irrelevant. On the most mundane level, this shift in orientation is due to the fact that by the late 1960s, most Nuyoricans were second-generation migrants raised in the barrio. Meanwhile, as salsa acquired a character distinct from that of a transplanted island music, New York became a more dynamic and internationally influential center for Latin music than provincial San Juan, or, for that matter, Cuba, which was by now isolated by the United States embargo. Above all, the period 1965-78—the heyday of "classic" salsa—witnessed a dramatic and unprecedented celebration and valorization of Nuyorican identity. In this period, salsa emerged as the voice of barrio youth with all their restless, alienated energy and exuberant optimism. As with the sense of "double consciousness" said to animate much of African-American culture, much of salsa's freshness and vigor derived precisely from the unique Nuyorican self-conception. Although marginalized in the barrio, Latino youth saw themselves as uniquely empowered to lead Latinos throughout the continent toward a new and glorious destiny. It is precisely this animating ideology, rather than stylistic differences, which came to distinguish salsa from what Rondon calls the "ingenuous and provincial" Cuban *guarachas* and *sones* from which it evolved (Rondón 1980, 64).

With salsa, Latin music became self-consciously rooted in New York as never before. Fania Records' 1971 promotional film *Our Latin Thing* rendered this identification explicit, juxtaposing concert footage with scenes of barrio street life. Several songs hailed New York as the crucible of Latin music. In "Salsa en Nueva York," Típica Novel (a *charanga* group) sang of the city as the *"cuna del ritmo y sabor"* ("cradle of rhythm and flavor"), and in "La Batalla de los Barrios" ("The Battle of the Barrios"), the group portrayed the city's boroughs vying for the distinction of producing the best salsa.[14] Willie Colon devoted an entire song, "Nueva York" to expressing his ambivalent fascination with the city:

> Nueva York, paisaje de acero,
> no sé si te odio, no sé si te quiero
> Cuando estoy contigo me siento inquieto por largarme
> Cuando estoy lejos loco por mirarte

Nueva York, selva de concreto
Mi corazón guarda el secreto, en tus labios latinos
Yo vi por primera vez las tradiciones de mis abuelos
Mágica ciudad de sueños dorados, capital de desilusiones
No sé cómo ni por qué me llevo embrujado,
Donde quiera me recuerdo de Nueva York...
Nueva York, ciudad palabrera, locura valiente, belleza turbia
Millones de seres juntos se sienten solos
Cuántos desventurados que no retornan...

New York, landscape of steel,
I don't know if I hate you or love you.
When I'm with you I want to flee,
when I'm away, I'm dying to see you.
New York, concrete jungle, my heart keeps the secret.
In your Latino lips, I saw for the first time
the traditions of my grandparents.
Magic city of golden dreams, capital of disillusionment
I don't know how or why you bewitch me.
I remember New York everywhere...
New York, verbose city, valiant madness, clouded beauty,
millions of people together feel lonely.
How many lost souls never return...[15]

In Conjunto Libre's "Imagenes Latinas" ("Latin Images"), New York is the site of the creative confluence of Latin American Indians, Blacks, and Hispanics, who merge to forge a new race with a common destiny. The conception of New York as the center of Latin music was similarly explicit in songs like "El Mensaje" ("The Message") recorded in 1975 by the New York-based band of Bobby Rodriguez:

Te traigo un mensaje...
Es que yo tengo la clave de este ritmo guaguancó...
sonido moderno de la isla del encanto
Yo le canto a mi Puerto Rico y a Los Angeles también
A Venezuela y Santo Domingo...

I bring you a message...
It's the *clave* of the *guaguancó* rhythm...
The modern sound from the enchanted isle [Puerto Rico].
I sing to my Puerto Rico, and to Los Angeles as well
to Venezuela and Santo Domingo...[16]

Here, the new sound is identified as the *guaguancó* (a traditional rumba style), depicted as coming from Puerto Rico (its Cuban origins being at this point essentially irrelevant; see Manuel 1994). Salsa is thus ambiguously linked to tradition, and to Puerto Rico, but it is essentially created in and disseminated from the new center of gravity, New York City, to the rest of the Latin world (excluding Cuba, which would be like bringing coals to Newcastle). And indeed, Venezuela, Colombia, and other regional sites have become new centers for salsa, which, in its classic period, evolved from being the defiant expression of local barrio alienation to the favored dance idiom of all urban classes.

Of particular prominence during this period were the song texts of Rubén Blades and Willie Colon, which examined barrio life in all its vitality and perversity. Although variously dubbed *"salsa consciente"* or "protest salsa," many such songs might in retrospect be called "gangster salsa" for their colorful portrayal of the violent and sordid underside of ghetto life. While Blades' "Numero Seis" was a light-hearted complaint about waiting for the subway, more typical were songs like Colon's "Calle Luna Calle Sol," which paints a portrait of ghetto malevolence and danger. Similarly, "Juanito Alimaña" depicts a rapacious and fearless hoodlum; "Juan Pachanga" (1977) exposes the inner emptiness and vapidity of a narcissistic dandy. "Pedro Najava" (1979), the most textually rich and musically innovative of all, presents a sort of existential snapshot of barrio life—one of "eight million New York stories"—in which a *guapo* and a hooker shoot each other:

> ...Y créanme gente, que aunque hubo ruido, nadie salió
> No hubo curiosos, no hubo preguntas, nadie lloró.
> Sólo un borracho con los dos muertos se tropezó
> cogió el revólver, el puñal, los pesos y se marchó.
>
> Y tropezando, se fue cantando desafina'o
> el coro que aquí les traje y da el mensaje de mi canción:
> "La vida te da sorpresas, sorpresas te da la vida, ¡Ay Dios!"

> And believe me folks, even though there was a noise,
> nobody came out to look.
> There were no curious onlookers, no questions, no one wept,
> just one drunk, who stumbled over the two corpses,
> pocketed the revolver, the dagger, their money and walked on.

And as he stumbled, he sang, out of tune,
the refrain that I'm bringing to you
and that's the message of my song:
"My goodness, life is full of surprises, isn't it?"[17]

These lyrics, despite salsa's primary function as dance music, enjoyed extraordinary popularity; "Pedro Navaja" alone inspired a long-
running Puerto Rican play, critical essays, and other songs (see
Arteaga Rodríguez 1988, 28-29), while "Juan Pachanga" became
the name of a Queens salsa club.

Of particular interest is the way that such songs situate New York
City as the center of an emergent, international Latino culture. On
one level, as Arteaga Rodríguez observes, they could be seen as per-
petuating the tradition of machismo and *guapería* found in old Cuban *sones* and the 1950s plenas and *bombas* of Rafael Cortijo
(Arteaga Rodríguez 1988, 22-24). The difference in terms of social
geography, however, is not merely that salsa songs were set (whether
explicitly or implicitly) in New York rather than in Havana or
Santurce. Rather, the distinguishing feature of salsa's *sabor* was
the self-consciousness with which it dramatized the urban experience. Although the barrio depicted was on one level marginal, in
other respects it was, as Rondón notes, "the fundamental element
which served to unite and identify the totality of Latin music in this
century" (Rondón 1980, 110). By 1970, most of the population of
the Spanish Caribbean Basin had become urban, and lumpen barrio life had become a new sort of international norm, however inherently peripheral to the economic mainstream. Salsa
self-consciously captured this sense of marginality and linked it to
a spirit of international Latino unity and mobilization. Thus, while
Rubén Blades situated his "Pedro Navaja" specifically in New York,
he clarified that he intended such songs to be "the folklore of the
city—not of one city, but of all the cities in Latin America" (Marre
and Charleton 1985, 80).

New York in the Global Soundscape

From the vantage point of the mid-1990s, the heyday of classic
salsa looks like a unique period. Today, New York *salseros* no longer
entertain the heady and messianic faith that their music will serve
as the voice for a united international Latino renaissance. Accordingly, New York is no longer celebrated as the unique epicenter of
Latin music. By the mid-1980s, indeed, the sociomusical configu-
ration that lent such vigor and optimism to barrio attitudes and to

salsa had changed dramatically, in ways that are subtly reflected in the presence—or absence—of New York City in Latin music texts.

One aspect of the new situation involves the very success of salsa, which, as predicted in songs like "El Mensaje," did indeed spread throughout the Caribbean Basin. Since Caracas, Cali, and other regional cities have come to host their own lively salsa scenes, New York can no longer claim to be the towering beacon of the salsa world; rather, in terms of market, creativity, and ideology, it is merely one center among several. Given the unprecedentedly international nature of the genre, there are fewer songs devoted to specific sites like New York (aside from merengues narrating the immigrant experience). Those that do exist are as likely to commemorate other cities (e.g., "Cali Pachanguero"), and may be written primarily to boost audiences on the tour circuit (just as the 1940s plena band of César Concepción devoted songs to Puerto Rican towns on its own smaller circuit).

Meanwhile, international popularity notwithstanding, salsa itself no longer enjoys the centrality it formerly held within the New York Latino community. If classic-era salseros envisioned their music as the dominant and integrating medium for Latino identity, the mid-1990s situation is characterized by what Juan Flores calls "an ever-broadening field of expressive practices" (1994, 90). Specifically, this would include the merengue boom, the ongoing attrition of Nuyorican would-be salsa fans to rock and hip hop, and, lastly, the emergence of Latin rap. The last might be in a position to serve as a new voice of the barrio, for its playful delight in Spanglish and urban hybridity place it at the cutting edge of postmodern subcultural expressivity. Latin rap pieces like Latin Empire's "En mi Viejo South Bronx" (sardonically invoking the sentimental mid-century bolero "En mi Viejo San Juan") could provide a fresh musical expression of New York life in music. Similarly, one of the few invocations of New York in contemporary salsa consists of an English-language, rock/rap-style "shout-out" to the boroughs by La India (Linda Caballero) in her "Llegó la India."[18] However, Latin rap remains a marginal genre, with little airplay in New York. Moreover, as Flores has observed, New York Latinos have yet to gain prominence in the field, which instead remains dominated by a remarkably international set of Chicanos, Central American immigrants, and Puerto Rican islanders (Flores 1994, 95-96).

In a subtle, yet ultimately more significant sense, the decline of references to New York City in Latin music since the 1970s reflects a dramatically changed socio-political ambience. The social-realist songs of Rubén Blades and Willie Colon were expressing more than a titillating fascination with gangsters. Rather, they were linked, whether explicitly or implicitly, with a sense of political activism and optimism. Within the United States the late 1960s and early 1970s was a period of rising economic expectations, a vigorous youth counterculture, the Civil Rights movement, and successful Nuyorican mobilizations by the Young Lords. Throughout the hemisphere, the left, however ferociously repressed, was actively challenging North American imperialism. Salsa songs chronicling barrio life were intimately connected to this sense of activism, idealism, and optimism. People like poet, salsa lyricist, and Young Lords leader Felipe Luciano envisioned salsa not as escapist entertainment but as an invigorating street music obliging Latinos to confront their social reality and, ultimately, to change it.[19]

Subsequent decades saw the defeat of the Latin American and Caribbean left, the fizzling of the counterculture and Civil Rights movements, the collapse of international socialism, and the renewed impoverishment of minorities and the lower classes by a triumphant Reaganism which remains undiluted, as of the mid-1990s. Accordingly, the fervent and sanguine idealism and social realism of classic salsa have given way to the glib ribaldry of merengue and what classic-era salseros regard as the slick sentimentality of modern *salsa romántica* (not to mention the nihilistic machismo so common in hardcore rap). References to New York City, or to lived social reality in general, find little place in modern Latin dance music, whose sole aim seems to be to divert rather than to mobilize or educate. As the morale and standard of living of minorities decline in the New World Order, the barrio and its problems seem to have disappeared both from song texts and from the concerns of the state. It remains to be seen if some new or reinvigorated form of Latin music, in tandem with a revitalized socio-political assertiveness, can again promote a sense of active engagement with the vital issues of contemporary urban life.

NOTES

1. "Un Jíbaro en Nueva York," Ansonia SALP 1537, recorded by Baltazar Carrero, reissued 1975. A partial text of El Gallito de Manatí's "Culpando el Subway" ("Lost on the Subway") is found in Manuel (1995, 66). These two songs, and the text cited below, "Yo me Quedo en Puerto Rico," are in ten-line *décima* form. Thanks to Edgardo Díaz for his assistance in translating some of the songs cited in this work.

2. "Yo me Quedo en Puerto Rico," Artillería 1030, recorded by Ramito (Florencio Morales Ramos). This recording appears to be an unauthorized compilation of earlier releases.

3. Cited in Cortes, Falcon, and Flores (1976, 125-26).

4. Cf., e.g., "Besando a Puerto Rico" (Ansonia SALP 1463).

5. Listen to, for example, Ramito's *seis* "Puerto Rico Cambiado" (Ansonia 1492), the Trío Vegabajeño's *guajira*-style bolero "Ven Jíbaro Ven" (Ansonia 1482), and Julito Rodríguez's "Besando a Puerto Rico" (Ansonia 1463).

6. The text is presented in full in Glasser (1995, 183-84).

7. "La Metrópolis," Ansonia SALP 1444, composed and recorded by Ismael Santiago.

8. "En la 116," Harlequin 2075, recorded by Los Reyes de la Plena, 1989.

9. "Un Jíbaro en Nueva York," on *Navidad Criolla*, INCA JMIS 1066, recorded by Sonora Ponceña, 1978.

10. "Nueva York es Así," Gema GCD-040, recorded by La Patrulla 15.

11. "El Hombre Llegó Para'o," Canela 409-2T, recorded by Pocho y su Cocobanda, 1995.

12. "Un Día en Nueva York," Karen 10793-0169-4, recorded by Los Hermanos Rosario, 1995.

13. "El Gringo y el Cibaeño," Karen KLP 87, recorded by Wilfrido Vargas, 1984.

14. "Salsa en Nueva York" and "La Batalla de los Barrios," TTH TR-121, recorded by Típica Novel, 1988.

15. "Nueva York," Fania 4XT-JM-00535, composed and recorded by Willie Colon, 1979.

16. "El Mensaje," Vaya V5-43, recorded by Bobby Rodriguez, 1976.

17. The full text of "Pedro Najava" is found on "Ruben Blades: The Best," Sony CDZ-80718, recorded by Ruben Blades, 1979. For full texts of most of the songs mentioned in the previous paragraph see Rondón (1980, 104, 313-16), Duany (1984), and Arteaga Rodríguez (1988). See also Randel (1991) and Cortes et

al (1976) for further discussion of these songs and their rela-
tion to the spirit of the decade. Recordings of Colon's "Juanito
Alimaña" and "Calle Luna Calle Sol" are found on "Vigilante,"
Fania JM 610, 1983, and "Willie Colon: Su Vida Musical,"
Profono TPL-402,1982, respectively.

18. "Llegó la India," Soho SHEC 80864, recorded by La India (Linda
Caballero).

19. See Felipe Luciano's statements in Marre and Charleton (1985,
80-83).

REFERENCES CITED

Aparicio, Frances. 1997. *Listening to Salsa: Gender, Latin Popular Music, and Puerto Rican Culture.* Hanover, NH: University Press of New England.

Arteaga Rodríguez, Jose. 1988. "Salsa y Violencia: Una Aproximación Sonoro Histórica." *Revista Musical Puertorriqueña* 4: 16-33.

Black, Jan Knippers. 1986. *The Dominican Republic: Politics and Development in an Unsovereign State.* Boston: Allen and Unwin.

Cortes, Felix, Angel Falcon, and Juan Flores. 1976. "The Cultural Expression of Puerto Ricans in New York: A Theoretical Perspective and Critical Review." *Latin American Perspectives* 3(3): 117-152.

Duany, Jorge. 1984. "Popular Music in Puerto Rico: Toward an Anthropology of Puerto Rican Music." *Latin American Music Review* 5(2): 186-215.

Flores, Juan. 1991. "Cortijo's Revenge." *Centro de Estudios Puertorriqueños Bulletin* 3(2): 8-21.

_____. 1994. "Puerto Rican and Proud, Boyee!: Rap, Roots and Amnesia." In *Microphone Fiends*, ed. Andrew Ross and Tricia Rose, 89-98. New York: Routledge.

Glasser, Ruth. 1995. *My Music Is My Flag: Puerto Rican Musicians and Their New York Communities 1917-1940.* Berkeley: University of California Press.

Lewis, Oscar. 1968. *La Vida: A Puerto Rican Family in the Culture of Poverty—San Juan and New York.* New York: Vintage Books.

Manuel, Peter. 1994. "Puerto Rican Music and Cultural Identity: Creative Appropriation of Cuban Sources from Danza to Salsa." *Ethnomusicology* 38(2): 249-80.

Manuel, Peter, with Kenneth Bilby and Michael Largey. 1995. *Caribbean Currents: Caribbean Music from Rumba to Reggae.* Philadelphia: Temple University Press.

Marre, Jeremy, and Hannah Charleton. 1985. *Beats of the Heart: Popular Music of the World.* New York: Pantheon.

Pacini Hernandez, Deborah. 1995. *Bachata: A Social History of Dominican Popular Music.* Philadelphia: Temple University Press.

Randel, Don. 1991. "Crossing Over with Rubén Blades." *Journal of the American Musicological Society* 44(2): 301-23.

Rondón, César. 1980. *El libro de la salsa: Crónica de la música del Caribe urbano.* Caracas.

Spottswood, Richard, and Cristóbal Díaz Ayala. 1989. Liner notes to *The Music of Puerto Rico* (Harlequin 2075).

From Transplant to Transnational Circuit
Merengue in New York

Paul Austerlitz

A car speeds down a Manhattan street, blasting flashy Latino saxophone riffs and pulsating drums. *Merengue*, the national music of the Dominican Republic, has become an integral part of New York City's contemporary soundscape. Surveying the social history of merengue, this essay contrasts the music's modest presence in New York in the 1950s with its current high-profile state.[1]

Traditional notions of migration invoke visions of displaced individuals forging new lives in alien environments. Lifeways of the home society are maintained, but they are out of place in the new setting (Basch et al. 1994, 3-4). Reyes-Schramm's and Qureshi's early studies of immigrant music cultures apply this perspective to ethnomusicology, regarding immigrant expressions as "transplants" of musical traditions from home societies (Reyes-Schramm 1989; Qureshi 1972, 38). The transplant model is useful when home and host societies are isolated from one another.[2] While such conditions might have been prevalent in the past, transnational capitalism and the information revolution mandate new approaches. Remittances, high rates of return migration, and telephone links fashion inextricable networks between host and home societies, which coalesce into what Rouse calls "single communit[ies] spread across a variety of sites," or "transnational migrant circuit[s]" (1991, 15; also see Basch et al. 1994; Glick Schiller et al. 1992; Marcus 1986). Merengue in New York began as a transplant and became a transnational circuit.

Dominican Merengue

The terms *merengue* (Spanish) and *mereng* (Haitian Creole) refer to related but stylistically distinct dance musics performed in several Caribbean countries, including the Dominican Republic, Haiti, Venezuela, and Colombia. Progeny of such European forms as the *contradanza*, Dominican merengue emerged during the mid-nineteenth century as elite, European-derived dance music became tinged with Afro-Caribbean elements. After a period of popularity in Dominican ballrooms, merengue was rejected by cosmopolitan upper-class Dominicans because of its African influences and suggestive dance style. The rural Dominican masses, however, adopted merengue, infusing it with even more African elements and performing it on instruments local to the various regions of the Republic. This practice gave rise to several stylistically distinct regional and rural variants of Dominican merengue.

Early twentieth-century *merengue típico cibaeño*, or rural merengue of the Cibao (north-central) region, was performed on the button accordion, the *tambora* drum (played with a stick in the right hand and the palm of the left hand), the metallic *güira* scraper, and sometimes, the alto saxophone. It was dance music played primarily at recreational dances, cock fights, and brothels. Accordionist/singer/composers Francisco "Ñico" Lora and Antonio "Toño" Abreu were the architects of twentieth-century merengue típico cibaeño, which served as the basis for subsequent nationally and internationally diffused merengue styles. To counteract United States hegemony during the 1916-24 occupation of the Dominican Republic, Cibao composers of European-style concert music such as Juan Francisco "Pancho" García and Julio Alberto Hernández drew upon rural merengue as raw material for a nationalist music. In a parallel move, such salon musicians as Luis Alberti combined merengue típico cibaeño instruments and rhythms with jazz-tinged North American big-band music.

Dominican dictator Rafael Trujillo rose to power in 1930. Like the European Fascists, Trujillo understood that expressive forms can serve as vital symbols for a nation-state. In 1936, he brought Luis Alberti's band, renamed Orquesta Presidente Trujillo, to the Republic's capital city to perform jazz-tinged big-band arrangements of merengue cibaeño at high-society balls. Trujillo required all the country's dance bands to perform newly composed merengues praising himself, and the mass media became an important channel for the diffusion of merengue. A rural, orally-transmitted regional ("folk") music performed primarily by the lower strata of society thus became an urban, mass-mediated commodified ("popular")

form and a national symbol associated with the elite but accessible
to all social groups. Other than Luis Alberti, the major exponent of
this national merengue style was Super Orquesta San José, directed
by Papa Molina and featuring Joseito Mateo (the "King of Merengue") on vocals and Tavito Vásquez on alto saxophone. In addition
to championing big-band merengue, Trujillo encouraged the transformation of accordion-based merengue típico cibaeño (which came
to be known as *perico ripiao*—ripped parrot) from a regional genre
into a national symbol.

Trujillo espoused a Hispanophilic, racist sense of national identity that rejected overtly African-influenced culture. Many Dominican rural musics associated with African-derived religious practices
were thus poor candidates for symbols of Trujilloist national identity. None the less, Trujillo considered merengue cibaeño appropriate as a national symbol, in spite of its African influences, because
of its historical acceptance by the Cibao upper class and its lack of
association with African-derived rituals.

A Transplanted National Music

Trujillo implemented an isolationist foreign policy; international
travel and contact with the outside world were closely regulated.
Fearing that Dominican musicians would not return, the dictator
rarely allowed them to perform outside of the country. Because of
this isolationism and a lack of recording opportunities in the Republic, Dominican merengue developed differently abroad than it
did at home.

The first Dominican musician to leave was bandleader Billo
Frómeta, who emigrated to Venezuela in 1936 (Alberti 1975, 75)
and founded a remarkably successful group called Billo's Caracas
Boys. Singer Alberto Beltrán moved to New York City in the late
1950s to work with the well-known group La Sonora Matancera.
Although he was primarily a *bolero* singer rather than a merengue
specialist, Beltrán popularized such merengues as "El Negrito del
Batey" and "Compadre Pedro Juan" among New York Latinos. Luis
Kalaff worked in Puerto Rico in 1956 and moved to New York City
in 1958, performing accordion-based merengue típico cibaeño first
at hotel shows and later at nightclubs for dancing (Kalaff 1990).
Also in New York, Negrito Chapuseaux and Rafael Damirón formed
a group that specialized in an "Americanized" merengue featuring
piano and maracas (Roberts 1979, 45), while Josecito Román and
Napoleon Zayas formed authentic merengue big bands. Merengue
gained popularity among New York City Latinos, and by the late
1950s it had found a permanent, although small, place in the reper-

tories of New York's Latin bands (Roberts 1979, 146; del Castillo and Arévalo 1989, 48).

Piano accordionist Angel Viloria moved to New York City in 1952 and established the single most successful merengue group outside of the Dominican Republic (Kalaff 1990). In spite of its name, Conjunto Típico Cibaeño, Viloria's group did not perform *típico* Cibao-style merengue. While its instrumentation of accordion, saxophone, and percussion was evocative of rural merengue, the Conjunto was modeled primarily on Luis Alberti's cosmopolitan sound. Like Alberti, Viloria utilized the piano accordion rather than the button accordion typical of rural merengue. The piano accordion was not suited to execute the percussive variations of the típico merengue, but its chromatic capabilities lent themselves to Alberti's jazz-influenced style. Viloria's use of the tenor rather than alto saxophone also set his band apart from merengue típico cibaeño. Most merengue groups in the Republic conformed either to the model set by salon bandleaders like Alberti or rural musicians like Ñico Lora. From a stylistic point of view, Viloria's group was notably dissimilar; a transplanted music, merengue was developing differently in New York than in its native environment.[3]

The Dominican community in the United States was small in the 1950s, and Viloria's audiences were predominantly Puerto Rican. As singer Joseito Mateo puts it, "it was the Puerto Ricans who originally brought merengue to popularity in New York, who gave their hand to merengue" (Mateo 1986). Mateo recalls that Puerto Rican men often attended dances to meet women, and that merengue dancing facilitated their quest. Merengue is danced in the ballroom position, and while couples may limit their physical contact to the arms, they may also press their bodies close together, making amorous contact. Mateo feels that this style made merengue appealing to Viloria's Puerto Rican fans in New York:

> El merengue es "música de ventaja," que da chance poder abrazar la mujer sin estar cometiendo nada malo...Para los dominicanos, es diferente:...el merengue es de figuraje, para la gente figuriar, para la gente estar bailando suelto. Pero los puertorriqueños prefieren el merengue lento, para ellos bailar pegaditos (Mateo 1986).

> Merengue is a music with which one can take advantage [of a woman]; it gives you a chance to embrace a woman without doing anything immoral. For Dominicans, it is different:...they dance merengue with figures and turns. But Puerto Ricans

like slow merengue, so that they can dance very close together (author's translation).

Viloria's merengue hit "La Ligadura" ("The Connection") refers simultaneously to the music's legato (connected) saxophone riffs and to the physical connection that men and women make while dancing.

Angel Viloria. Photo courtesy of Ansonia Records.

While the transnationalization of popular culture makes obsolete Turnstall's argument that "the media are American" (1977), Latin-Caribbean music long radiated from the United States. Salsa promoter George Nenadich is on the mark: "everything happens through New York: music, fashion, food;...merengue became popular in the outside world through New York" (Nenadich 1990). Trujillo held an iron grip on all aspects of the Dominican economy, including the music industry, which stressed live radio performances rather than recording. The paucity of recording opportunities for *merengueros* in the Republic limited the international exposure of music from the island. On the other hand, Angel Viloria's recordings on Ansonia Records were widely disseminated, and his transplanted music became the best-known manifestation of merengue outside of the Dominican Republic.

Viloria was especially popular in Cuba, where merengue became associated with Carnival. This vogue resulted in the development of Eduardo Davidson's *pachanga*, a new Cuban genre that combined merengue-style percussion rhythms with dance steps borrowed from the *guaracha* (Orovio 1991).[4] In Haiti, radio broadcasts and occasional tours of bands from the Dominican Republic generated audiences for Dominican merengue. However, it was Angel Viloria who established merengue in Haiti, as a local recording engineer remembers: "That thing hit like a bomb. The Haitians loved the merengue because it had a lively beat for dancing. They were doing it in every nightclub..." (H. Widmaier in Averill 1989, 104). Merengue became so popular in Haiti that it exerted a formative influence on the development of *konpa*, contemporary Haitian popular music (Averill 1989, 104-105). Moreover, Trujillo's use of merengue as propaganda may have inspired Haitian dictator Duvalier to make similar use of konpa. The cleavage between merengue in New York and at home is underlined by the fact that although Viloria was the top merenguero internationally, he was not especially popular in his native land. Because he was based in New York City, Viloria gained greater international exposure and exerted greater international influence than did merengueros based in the Dominican Republic.

Merengue and the Dominican Diaspora

After Trujillo was slain in 1961, Dominican-based bandleader Johnny Ventura incorporated *salsa* elements and a rock 'n' roll–influenced stage presence into a new, faster merengue.[5] In 1965, the United States again invaded the Dominican Republic. The period following the occupation was characterized by mixed feelings about this powerful neighbor to the north: on the one hand, the United States represented modernization and democracy; on the other hand, it had violated Dominican sovereignty. Ventura's merengue expressed this ambivalence, fusing rock and salsa with traditional merengue, thus providing a native alternative to the encroachment of transnational popular culture.

In the decades that followed, the Republic and the United States forged stronger links. Dominican President Balaguer's courting of North American capitalism led to foreign domination of all major private sectors of the Dominican economy. For example, from the 1960s through the 1980s the Gulf and Western Corporation invested so heavily in the Republic that some called the country a "company state" (Black 1986, 8-10). Beginning around 1965, changes in United States immigration law, combined with repressive political policies, unemployment, and high inflation in the Dominican Republic caused massive out-migration of Dominicans to New York City and Puerto Rico, Venezuela, and elsewhere. By 1990, close to 900,000 Dominicans were estimated to be living in New York City (Moya Pons 1995, 436). United States dollars earned by Dominican immigrants and sent to the Republic played an increasingly important role in the Dominican economy. Georges estimates that by the mid-1980s, remittances accounted for ten percent of the Dominican GDP gross domestic product almost equaling the earnings of the country's chief export industry, sugar (Georges 1990, 236). During a recession in 1990, a Dominican leftist concluded that the national economy was "kept alive thanks to the remittances sent by Dominicans living abroad" (Isa Conde in Féliz 1990, 13).

Merengue became central to Dominican life in the diaspora, and also found fans among non-Dominicans. In the early 1960s Primitivo Santos became the first Dominican bandleader to settle in the United States in the post-Trujillo era. Santos stayed with a fairly conservative style of merengue all through the 1960s and 1970s, neglecting currents of change. After living and working in New York for over twenty years, Santos moved back to the island in 1985. Interestingly, it was only immediately before his move that he began to utilize contemporary merengue innovations. Although Joseito Mateo never made a permanent move to New York, he worked there steadily from 1963, when he sang with Luis Kalaff at Club Caborojeño. In 1967, Mateo, Alberto Beltrán, and Primitivo Santos brought merengue to Madison Square Garden for the first time; Mateo regards this as a rite of passage symbolizing the arrival of merengue as an international phenomenon (Mateo 1986). A New York-born Dominican, Johnny Pacheco, who had led Latin bands in the City since the early 1960s, introduced merengue to many Latin Americans in the United States. While he specialized in salsa, Pacheco included the merengue "Los Diablitos" on his 1973 LP *Tres de Café y Dos de Azúcar*. Other *salseros* began to record merengue, and by 1976 merengue had reached a level of popularity among New York Latinos that was surpassed only by salsa (Rondón 1980, 29).

The growth of New York's Dominican community spawned merengue groups native to the City. The premier merengue band to come out of New York was Millie, Jocelyn y los Vecinos (Millie, Jocelyn, and the Neighbors). Led by siblings Millie and Jocelyn (lead singers) and Rafael (lead trumpeter, musical director, and arranger) Quezada, they started as amateurs in 1973, playing informally at neighborhood parties. Two years later the group turned professional and recorded its first LP. Millie Quezada remembers that in those early days, Los Vecinos provided "Dominican Yorks" (as Dominican New Yorkers were known on the island) with a link to their mother country:

> The nostalgic effect—that's the reason that Los Vecinos were formed. We really were very nostalgic. We didn't have any of the language or anything. And so, we kind of were trying to keep our roots, and out of that, the group was born. It was really out of a need, not only us, but the people in our neighborhood, to kind of stay in tune with what was happening with our music and with our cultural background in general...That's why we called the group Los Vecinos [The Neighbors] (Quezada 1990).

Dominican author Canelo agrees that merengue in New York's Dominican community is the single most important "physical-cultural" link that ties it to the Dominican Republic (1982, 33). Millie, Jocelyn y los Vecinos began to gain popularity outside of New York City in 1982, with hits in the United States, the Dominican Republic, Colombia, and Panama. They continue to be active, and maintain a high level of popularity.

Aside from Millie, Jocelyn, y los Vecinos, the two most successful merengue bands to emerge in New York referred to their hometown in their names, possibly as a marketing strategy. La Gran Manzana (The Big Apple) was notable for its innovative use of synthesizers and its inclusion of Haitian materials. The other group, called New York Band, performed Latin American romantic *baladas* and Trinidadian *soca*-influenced merengues. It featured four singers, each with his/her own solo vocal style. As creative artists, New York merengue musicians participated in the development of contemporary Dominican music. However, their styles did not differ qualitatively from the styles of groups in the Dominican Republic; like the Dominican economy, merengue had become transnational.

The Transnational Merengue Circuit

During the 1970s, merengue innovators in the Republic took the style farther down the path upon which Johnny Ventura had placed it—the music became a site for the domestication of outside elements. When disco became popular, merengue incorporated disco rhythms and drum machines, and when Latin American romantic baladas became popular, merengue utilized balada-type melodies and arrangements. Konpa, rap, Central African *soukous*, and other internationally-diffused popular musics also influenced merengue. Salsa promoter Nenadich attests that this vibrant new merengue sound became popular internationally during a period when salsa's popularity had ebbed:

> What happened was that around 1978, salsa was going through a total downfall. Sales came to a stop, and it became boring and repetitious. And merengue came in with such flair and such excitement. And the artists were completely different and it revived the generation. Plus, it was something new for the new generation of Latinos that were listening to tropical [Latin Caribbean] music. It was sort of like a light that came into the darkness (Nenadich 1990).

By the mid-1980s, merengue had usurped salsa's position as New York's number-one Latin dance. The *Village Voice* proclaimed that "besieged by merengue...salsa is going through hard times" (Fernández 1986, 18), and *Time* magazine reported that "a new merengue craze heats up the dance scene" taking up "a slackening interest in salsa" (Cocks 1986). Merengue's popularity among non-Dominicans was often credited to its easy-to-learn dance style. After taking a whirl on the dance floor, New York's Mayor Koch said that "[t]his is the one dance that you can do from the moment you're born" (in Cocks 1986). As in the 1950s, the sexual element contributed to merengue's popularity—*Time* magazine noted that "partners can press hips close enough to grind grain" (Cocks 1986).

Promoter Nenadich asserts that New York served as a conduit for merengue's popularity all over Latin America and beyond, pointing out that "during that time period, when salsa was falling, it also fell across the sea. In Spain, it just died. And when merengue came in [to New York], it came in with the same kind of flair in Europe, in Japan, in South America" (Nenadich 1990). Merengue's incorporation of sundry musical styles played an important role in making the music appealing to new audiences. Balada elements likely appealed to South American audiences, while rap and disco influences attracted New York City Latino youth. Bandleader Juan Luis Guerra proclaims that:

> El merengue está a punto de convertirse a una música que se da oír en todo el mundo, por primera vez por eso: ahora está más fácil a la gente a oírlo, sobre todo a los extranjeros (Guerra 1986).

> Merengue is in a position to become a music heard throughout the world now, because now it is easier for people to listen to it, especially for foreigners (author's translation).

Merengue's international popularity grew in spite of, rather than through the efforts of, the established New York City Latin music industry. This industry failed to actively promote merengue, partly because it felt that the Dominican Republic is not a lucrative market (Nenadich 1990), but also because the Puerto Ricans, Cuban-Americans, and Italian-Americans who dominated the music business did not have a nationalist interest in promoting Dominican music. Some have charged that the New York's Latin music industry actually worked against Dominican music. For example, Dominican deejay Willie Rodríguez claimed that the powerful New York Latin music company Fania "boycotted" merengue, not only in New York City and Puerto Rico, but even in the Dominican Republic (Rodríguez 1986, 17). One non-Dominican music promoter in New York City (who wished to remain anonymous) said that "we don't manage any merengue artists; tropical [Latin Caribbean] music is still divided in this sense." Perhaps referring to misunderstandings between New York promoters and merengue musicians, he added that "we used to book merengue, but due to mishaps, we closed it down." To some Dominicans, merengue's international success represented vindication of this situation; Rodríguez said that merengueros are "guerrillas of the music, who go to Puerto Rico and place a bomb in the places that they play" (1986, 21).

Merengue's popularity among non-Dominicans resulted in the founding of merengue bands by non-Dominicans. I played the saxophone with non-Dominican (as well as Dominican) merengue bands in the New York metropolitan area for several years. When performing with a Central American band in the early 1980s, I was struck by the popularity of Dominican music; dancers were sparse when we played Honduran and Salvadorian *cumbias*, but they filled the floor as soon as we began a merengue. During the early 1980s,

Puerto Rican bands in Connecticut specialized in salsa. The bands did not keep pace with recent developments in Dominican music, and the few merengues in their repertories were often "oldies" dating to the 1950s. By the late 1980s, however, most Connecticut Latin bands specialized in merengue, duplicating the latest innovations of Dominican music.

Merengue and Transnational Identities

A German politician, irritated by the independent style of guest-worker communities, once complained that "We called for workers, and we got people" (Grasmuck and Pessar 1991, 208). As Grasmuck and Pessar note, "labor is not comparable to the other commodities that are exchanged on a global scale" (1991, 208). Migrants are part of the transnational economy, but they negotiate circumstances and forge multiple identities according to their own agendas. The transnational merengue style that Johnny Ventura and Wilfrido Vargas created played a significant role in the development of contemporary "Dominicanness" both in the diaspora and on the island. Like the Nigerian musicians that Christopher Waterman has written about, merengueros are culture brokers: "[P]ositioned at important interstices in heterogeneous urban societies, they [culture brokers] forge new styles and communities of taste, negotiating cultural differences through the musical manipulation of symbolic associations (Waterman 1990, 9). The domestication of world musics within the rubric of an avowedly *Dominican* merengue rendered the music's aesthetic space into what Paredes calls a "border-zone," or "sensitized area where...cultures come face to face" (Paredes 1978, 68).

Merengue is a prime marker of ethnic identity for Dominicans in New York City. As one Dominican New Yorker explains, "We're very proud of our merengue. I was dancing merengue since I was two years old. At the same time that I learned to walk, I was learning to dance merengue" (in Echevarría 1991). I once asked a Dominican teenager in New York what kind of music she likes. She answered that she liked "American" music. I pressed, asking her whether she cared for Latin music: salsa and merengue. She answered that salsa was not much to her liking but that "of course I like merengue. I'm Dominican." My impression was that although merengue was not her preferred style, she considered it a patriotic duty to speak well of the national music.

Connections between Dominicans in New York and those in the Dominican Republic are so pervasive as to have strongly influenced Dominican identity, even on the island. In addition to the economic dependency, a "psychic dependency" between Dominicans in the two places generated mania for emigration (Grasmuck and Pessar 1991, 16); Dominicans came to say that island-dwellers are *"loco para irse,"* or "obsessed with the idea of emigrating" (Bray 1987, 64). Grasmuck and Pessar encountered a poignant expression of Dominican transnational identity in a photograph sent by a rural Dominican woman to her husband in New York, who had supported his family through remittance dollars for many years. In order to express the well-being of the family and its debt to the father, the woman dressed her sons in borrowed suits and traveled to the nearest city to have the photo taken in a studio. The family posed in front of a backdrop of the Brooklyn Bridge (Grasmuck and Pessar 1991, 7).

Identifying with both the Dominican Republic and the United States can be disorienting. Former Dominican President Balaguer once called diaspora Dominicans *"los dominicanos ausentes"* ("absent Dominicans"). Millie Quezada claims the physical absence extends to a feeling of being lost between two cultures. "Balaguer has called us absent Dominicans," she explains, "we're kind of in nowhereland. I feel that we, as Dominicans living outside, are *more* Dominican because we kind of miss the homeland" (Quezada 1990). Noting what she considers an identity crisis among New York-born Puerto Ricans, Quezada sees Dominicans facing similar problems:

> Third and fourth generation of Puerto Ricans have lost, are losing, their language, are losing their heritage. They're going through some kind of turmoil about who they really are, they are Americans or they are Puerto Ricans [*sic*]. That's going to happen with the Dominicans (Quezada 1990).

She continues, affirming the role that merengue plays in shaping cultural identities on the cusp of the transnational circuit:

> We're trying to do something to keep what we have, because to lose your identity is kind of, it's kind of rough. Living in the United States is, you don't belong here, and you're not there, so you're kind of in limbo...We make a point of keeping the music and of telling the people who we are. We can survive here. Not just survive, but make something of ourselves, and at the same time, be proud of who we were, where we came from. It's a big deal for us (Quezada 1990).

But Quezada does not consider the music a static repository of "tradition," trusting instead that its use of non-Dominican elements will render it relevant to life in the United States. She extends this hope to non-Dominican Latinos as well as to Dominicans:

> [By incorporating these influences] we are trying to...capture the generations of Hispanics that are kind of being lost to rock, to other kinds of music. We want them to kind of keep looking for their roots. We're hoping that continues, and so we're trying to rescue them. To keep the youth (Quezada 1990).

While merengue does represent pan-Latino identity to some non-Dominicans, my experiences indicate that this is less true in New York City than in Puerto Rico, Connecticut, and the midwestern United States. In New York, ethnic boundaries between Latino groups are tightly drawn, and merengue most often marks Dominican rather than pan-Latino identity. When I was beginning to perform in New York Latin bands, a Puerto Rican friend once said, "Look across the street there, see that building? That's a Dominican building; almost everyone that lives in there is Dominican." Like most English-speaking New Yorkers, I was unable to distinguish the various Hispanic groups. I asked, "How do you know?" He answered, "Well, it's hard to say, exactly; they are just *different* [from us Puerto Ricans]. For one thing, they are always playing those merengue records."

Merengue's high profile on the global stage has bolstered its viability as an enduring national symbol in the Republic as well as among Dominicans in the diaspora. As Quezada puts it:

> I think that [Dominicans] are very proud to know that merengue has escalated into what it is today because, first of all, it makes the country known, because people want to know where is our music coming from, so it's a way of advertising the country. And also, I tend to think that they kind of feel a sense of pride to think that their music has been able to be assimilated by other countries. You know, that's not something that happens quite often (Quezada 1990).

Merengue is part of the fabric of New York. Like the histories of mambo and salsa, the story of merengue in New York tells of an "implosion of the Third World into the first" (Rosaldo 1988, 85, cited in Rouse 1991, 17). As a Finnish-born New Yorker whose life has been deeply touched by performing and researching merengue, I can attest to the force of this implosion.

NOTES

1. This paper draws on materials found in the author's recently published work, *Merengue: Dominican Music and Dominican Identity* (Austerlitz 1997). The author gratefully acknowledges the Wenner-Gren Foundation for Anthropological Research, which supported field research in the Dominican Republic in 1990-91 and 1995.

2. Such isolation is rare. Even European immigrants to the United States in the early and middle twentieth century influenced music in their countries of origin. For example, the Finnish immigrant community in the United States played an important role in the development of popular music in Finland. Contrasting Boasian "old ethnicity," which was developed in studies of relatively isolated, homogeneous societies, with border-zone "new ethnicity," developed in studies of contemporary pluralistic societies, Bennett (1973:3-4) argues that their difference may be attributable as much to epistemological shifts in academia as to changes in human behavior. Goldberg notes that border-zone immigrant identities were celebrated already in 1916, when *Atlantic Monthly* writer Randolph Bourne called for United States citizens to "make something out of this trans-national spirit instead of outlawing it" (in Glick Schiller et al 1992:212). However, jet-age travel and the information revolution have caused fundamental changes, to the extent that the current situation is qualitatively different from that faced by earlier migrants.

3. However, Viloria's group was not unique; groups with piano accordion and saxophone frontlines also existed in the Dominican Republic.

4. The Cuban pachanga was different from the pachanga that developed in New York City in the early 1960s. The latter took its name from the Cuban pachanga, but was stylistically related to the *cha-cha-chá* and *charanga* rather than to merengue (see Thompson 1961).

5. Arranger Luis Pérez played an important role in forging these innovations.

REFERENCES CITED

Alberti, Luis. 1975. *De música y orquestas bailables dominicanas, 1910-1959*. Santo Domingo: Taller.

Austerlitz, Paul. 1986. "A History of Dominican Merengue Highlighting the Role of the Saxophone." M.A. thesis, Wesleyan University.

_____. 1992. "Dominican Merengue in Regional, National, and International Perspectives." Ph.D. dissertation, Wesleyan University.

_____. 1993. "Local and International Trends in Dominican Merengue." *World of Music* 35: 270-89.

_____. 1997. *Merengue: Dominican Music and Dominican Identity*. Philadelphia: Temple University Press.

Averill, Gage. 1989. "Haitian Dance Band Music: The Political Economy of Exuberance." Ph.D. dissertation, University of Washington.

Basch, Linda, Nina Glick Schiller, and Cristina Szanton Blanc. 1994. *Nations Unbound: Transnational Projects, Postcolonial Predicaments, and Deterritorialized Nation-States*. Basel: Gordon and Breach Publishers.

Bennett, John W., ed. 1973. *The New Ethnicity*. St. Paul: West Publishing Company.

Black, Jan Knippers. 1986. *The Dominican Republic: Politics and Development in an Unsovereign State*. Boston: Allen and Unwin.

Bray, David B. 1987. "Dominican Exodus: Origins, Problems, Solutions." In *Caribbean Exodus*, ed. Barry Levine. New York: Praeger.

Canelo, Juan de Frank. 1982. *Dónde, por qué, como viven los dominicanos en el extranjero*. Santo Domingo: Editora Alpha y Omega.

Cocks, Jay. 1986. "You Can't Stop Dancing: A New Merengue Heats Up the Club Scene." *Time* (6 October): 91.

del Castillo, José and Manuel A. García Arévalo. 1989. *Antología del Merengue/Anthology of the Merengue*. Santo Domingo: Editora Corripio.

Echevarría, Vito. 1991. "Santo Domingo on the Hudson." *Hispanic* 32 (September): 38.

Féliz, José Miguel. 1990. "Isa Conde destaca aportes de dominicanos que residen en el exterior." *Actualidad/Listin Diario* 17 (Diciembre): 13.

Fernández, Enrique. 1986. "Is Salsa Sinking?" *Village Voice* (2 September): 18, 20-21.

Georges, Eugenia. 1990. *The Making of a Transnational Community: Migration, Development and Cultural Change in the Dominican Republic*. New York: Columbia University Press.

Glick Schiller, Nina, Linda Basch, and Cristina Blanc-Szanton, eds. 1992. *Towards a Transnational Perspective on Migration*. New York: The New York Academy of Sciences.

Grasmuck, Sherri, and Patricia R. Pessar. 1991. *Between Two Islands: Dominican International Migration*. Berkeley: University of California Press.

Guerra, Juan Luis. 1986. Personal interview with the author.

Kalaff, Luis. 1990. Personal interview with the author.

Marcus, George E. 1986. "Contemporary Problems of Ethnography in the Modern World System." In *Writing Culture: The Poetics and Politics of Identity*, ed. James Clifford and George E. Marcus. Berkeley: University of California Press.

Mateo, Joseito. 1986. Personal interview with the author.

Moya Pons, Frank. 1995. *The Dominican Republic: A National History*. New Rochelle, NY: Hispaniola Books.

Nenadich, George. 1990. Personal interview with the author.

Orovio, Helio. 1991. Personal communication with the author.

Paredes, Américo. 1978. "The Problem of Identity in a Changing Culture: Popular Expressions of Culture Conflict along the Rio Grande Border." In *Views Across the Border: The United States and Mexico*, ed. Stanley R. Ross. Albuquerque: University of New Mexico Press.

Quezada, Millie. 1990. Personal interview with the author.

Qureshi, Regula. 1972. "Ethnomusicological Research among Canadian Communities of Arab and East Indian Origin." *Ethnomusicology* 16(3): 381-96.

Reyes-Schramm, Adelaida. 1989. "Music and Tradition from Native to Adopted Land through the Refugee Experience." *Yearbook for Traditional Music* 22: 25-35.

Roberts, John Storm. 1979. *The Latin Tinge*. New York: Oxford University Press.

Rodríguez, Willie. 1986. "Impactos de las orquestas populares en la programación de las radio-emisoras del país." *Acroarte: Primer seminario sobre las orquestas populares en nuestro país* 1(1):15-26.

Rondón, César Miguel. 1980. *El libro de la salsa: Crónica de la música del caribe urbano*. Caracas: Ed. Arte.

Rosaldo, Renato. 1988. "Ideology, Place, and People without Culture." *Cultural Anthropology* 3(1): 77-87.

Rouse, Roger. 1991. "Mexican Migration and the Social Space of Postmodernism." *Diaspora* 1(1): 8-23.

Thompson, Robert Farris. 1961. "Portrait of the Pachanga: The Music, the Players, the Dancers." *Saturday Review* 44 (28 October): 42-43, 54.

Turnstall, Jeremy. 1977. *The Media Are American*. New York: Columbia University Press.

Waterman, Christopher. 1990. *Juju: A Social History and Ethnography of an African Popular Music*. Chicago: University of Chicago Press.

Recapturing History
The Puerto Rican Roots of Hip Hop Culture[1]

Juan Flores

Word has it that Machito, the father of Latin jazz, was learning how to breakdance at the age of seventy-five, shortly before his death in early 1984. The great Cuban bandleader who for decades stood at the juncture of Caribbean and African-American musical expression must surely have recognized an exciting new stage in the dual heritage he had made his own. For break and rap rhythms, with all their absorption of intervening and adjoining styles, remain grounded in African musical expression. They are further testimony to the shared cultural life of African-descended peoples in New York City, which for the past generation, at least, has centered on the interaction of Puerto Ricans and African Americans.

The proximity of the two groups is perhaps more striking today than ever before, especially among teenage youth. Aside from some studies of language convergence, the voluminous literature on ethnic relations in the United States includes no sustained treatment of the interaction between Puerto Ricans and African Americans in the United States. Perhaps the "pop" ascendancy of hip hop culture, which stems directly from this interaction, will provide a needed impetus.

The intellectual antecedents of this association predate Machito, dating back to the early 1900s, when the first contingents of Puerto Ricans began arriving in New York. They were mostly artisans, with a high level of political education, and many were black. Though Cubans and other Spanish speakers were their most immediate co-workers, African Americans were already a significant presence in their neighborhoods and work places. One of these very early arrivals was Arturo Alfonso Schomburg, who came to New York in the late nineteenth century. Unknown to many, he was Puerto Rican, and in fact dedicated the first period of his immigrant life to the Cuban and Puerto Rican struggle against Spanish colonialism. Early on in this century he moved up to Harlem, there to become one of the foremost scholars of the African diaspora. His contribution has been memorialized in Harlem's Schomburg Center for Research in Black Culture.

Another black Puerto Rican pioneer, who came to New York in 1917, was Jesús Colón. A longtime journalist and revolutionary activist, Colón in his literary sketches and political campaigns stressed the common historical and cultural experience of Puerto Ricans and African Americans. Writing in the 1940s and 1950s, he was the first Puerto Rican author to publish a book in English, and the first to describe in psychological detail his experience of American racism (Colón 1961).

An early admirer of Jesús Colón was the Puerto Rican novelist Piri Thomas, and here we draw closer to the contemporary world of hip hop. Thomas's *Down These Mean Streets* (1967), a work of autobiographical fiction in the style of Richard Wright's *Native Son* and Claude Brown's *Manchild in the Promised Land*, masterfully probes the complex and not always harmonious relations between African American and Puerto Rican youth in New York City. Here, in scenes set in the 1950s, we witness a young Puerto Rican saying the dozens and hanging out with his black friends; from them he learns that, according to the color code operative in the United States, he is black and had better start liking it.

With such hints of a longer historical trajectory in mind, it is to this period of the late 1950s and the 1960s that the origins of present-day hip hop culture must be traced. The spectacular surface of Broadway and Hollywood would have one think of *West Side Story* and *Blackboard Jungle*, the scenes of gang wars, drugs, and juvenile delinquency. A more circumspect account would recall that these years saw the dawning of the second-generation black and Puerto Rican communities in New York City; this was the time when the first offspring of both migrations, many of them born and raised in New York, were settling into their new situation. African Americans and Puerto Ricans comprised then, as they do today, the two largest nonwhite groups in the city. Both came from largely rural backgrounds, lived in the same or bordering neighborhoods, attended the same schools, and together occupied the most deprived and vulnerable place in the economic and cultural hierarchy: they were the reserve of the reserve.

Small wonder that young African Americans and Puerto Ricans started liking the same kinds of music, doing the same dances, playing the same games, and dressing and talking alike. Their common experience of racist exclusion and social distance from their white-ethnic peers drew them even closer together. In groping for a new idiom, young Blacks and Puerto Ricans discarded rural trappings and nostalgic "down home" references, but retained the African rhythmic base and improvisational, participatory qualities of their inherited cultures. In so doing, African-American and Caribbean peoples came to recognize the commonality of what seemed to be diverse origins.

One such intersection of the popular cultures was evident in rhythm-and-blues music of the late 1950s. Although both Fats Domino and Bo Diddley had already infused Latin and Caribbean beats into their influential rock 'n' roll sounds, New York was really the site of direct black and Puerto Rican musical interaction. Here street-based groups like the Harptones and the Vocaleers, and hugely successful acts like Frankie Lymon and the Teenagers, combined black and Latin members. The music, though basically African-American rock 'n' roll, included subtle *mambo* rhythms and other Afro-Caribbean features. The Latin influence was even stronger in the boogaloo craze led by Pete Rodríguez, Joe Cuba, and Joe Bataan during the late 1960s (Roberts 1979, 166-170; Salazar 1992).

Of course this analysis of commercial recordings takes into account only the "studio version" of what thousands of young Puerto Ricans and African Americans were singing in the streets, schoolyards, and hallways. Starting in the late 1950s and extending through the 1960s, vocal group rhythm-and-blues (or doo-wop) prevailed in the same neighborhoods that later gave rise to rap music. While the two vocal traditions exhibited stylistic differences—most notably rap's favoring of melodic chant over group harmonizing—vocal group rhythm-and-blues clearly prefigures rap musical practice in significant ways. The early street versions of both styles were performed by small vocal ensembles that alternated lead singers and employed minimal (if any) instrumental accompaniment. And like rap, vocal group rhythm-and-blues was a form of black urban music that was accessible to young Latin musicians, as a recording of Totico y Sus Rumberos singing "What's Your Name" illustrates. It's a "doo-wop *rumba*," and as Totico and his group recall, it fits perfectly.

The rap music that emerged in the late 1970s belongs squarely in the blues-derived, African-American tradition which relies heavily upon verbal dexterity in English. Yet similarities to Puerto Rican vocal styles are worth noting. Recital of Puerto Rican *décimas* and *aguinaldos* involve methods of improvisation and alternation much like those typical of rap performance, while the tongue-twisting (*trabalengua*) style of some *plena* singing is an even more direct antecedent. Perhaps more importantly, just as with vocal group rhythm-and-blues and rumba, there is a fascinating "fit" between Puerto Rican clave and characteristic rap rhythms. One of the earliest Puerto Rican rappers, Rubie Dee (Rubén García), who started off in street music as a *conguero* and a lover of *salsa*, illustrated this congruence to me. Dee, the Puerto Rican emcee from the Fantastic Five, was one of the first to rap in Spanish, while his brother Orlando composed bilingual "Spanglish" rhymes for the Funky Four. Other Puerto Ricans including Charlie Chase (Carlos Mandes) of the Cold Crush Brothers, TNT (Tomás Robles), and KMX Assault (Jenaro Díaz) were veterans of New York rap's early street days.

Graffiti-writing, the visual expression of hip hop culture, also reflects strong Puerto Rican influences. Although the best known early subway graffiti artists were from different national origins, many, including Lee Quiñones, Mono, and Doc of the now legendary Fabulous Five group, were Puerto Rican (Castleman 1982, 2-17; Hager 1984, 59). In 1972, when City College sociology student Hugo Martínez organized the first formal association to promote graffiti, the United Graffiti Artists, his initial members were almost entirely Puerto Rican (Castleman 1982, 117; Hager 1984, 25-27). Color and ecological aesthetics also come into play, as Norman Mailer suggested in 1974 when he described early New York graffiti art as "a movement which began as the expression of tropical peoples living in a monotonous, iron-gray and dull brown brick environment, surrounded by asphalt, concrete and clangor." Mailer goes on to suggest that graffiti "erupted biologically as though to save the sensuous flesh of their inheritance from a macadamization of the psyche, save the blank city wall of their unfed brain by painting the wall over with the giant trees and pretty plants of a tropical rain forest" (Mailer 1974).

Equally significant are the Puerto Rican contributions to the art of breakdancing. According to pioneer breaker Dennis Vázquez (the original "Rubber Band Man"), the early 1970s "up-rock" style danced to James Brown's "Sex Machine" and Jimmy Castor's "Just Begun" was a key innovation in the development of breakdancing (Vázquez 1983). The speedy footwork, elaborate upper-body movement, and daring dips in up-rock rested on a formative background in rumba and mambo, and was to some extent also anticipated by the Latin hustle. Many of the early Bronx breakdance crews including the Rockwell Association were made up of Puerto Ricans, and when young African Americans began moving on to other dances in the late 1970s, it was Puerto Rican breakers who rejuvenated the style (Hager 1984, 81-90). The Rock Steady Crew, one of the most accomplished breakdance groups of the 1980s and featured in the hip hop documentary film *Style Wars*, was composed almost entirely of Puerto Ricans. Input from other sources having more to do with African-American experience—martial arts, the jitterbug, tap dancing, and African social dance—has been duly noted, and the performance styles of James Brown and Frankie Lymon were of course key models. But the impulse toward a radical change in the physical center of gravity in popular dance and toward a "break" in the formalization of couple dancing seems to follow largely from developments in Latin dance styles.

TWI Crew, breakdancing on the Upper West Side, early 1980s.
Photo by Máximo Colón.

Such, then, are a few of the many forerunners and early manifestations of the triple-form style called hip hop. Of course this is not to suggest that rap, graffiti and breakdancing are not qualitatively new modes of cultural practice. On the contrary, the innovations brought to each area of popular expression are substantial indeed. Gaining a sense of historical background is mainly important in countering the dominant media's portrayal of these practices as stylistic novelties that sprang suddenly from thin air. Rather, all aspects of hip hop belong to the ongoing traditions of African-American and Puerto Rican experience, and to their convergence and cross-fertilization in the New York setting.

• • • •

Given this history it is surprising, and indeed troubling, that New York-based, Puerto Rican artists have not played a more prominent role in the burgeoning of commercial rap music in the 1980s and the emergence of Latin rap in the 1990s. Ironically, when rap went big-time in the mid-1980s, signs of Puerto Rican presence were all but erased. Of course they were there, even in high-profile groups like the Fat Boys, Cold Crush Brothers, and Master Don and the Def Committee, but their invisibility and anonymity as Puerto Ricans were complete; only a fraction of the public had any idea of their background. Needless to say, they were still very much there in the streets, and continued to contribute to the history of the genre under its rapidly changing conditions. But in the public eye, trained as it was on commercial film, video and concert fare, they were hidden in the woodwork, their historical role as co-creators totally occluded.

Charlie Chase, a pioneering Nuyorican DJ who began his career as a bass player in Latin dance bands, is a case in point. DJ Charlie was the musical foundation for the Cold Crush Brothers, the first rap group to be signed by CBS Records following a stellar appearance in the first hip hop movie, *Wild Style*. But as a Puerto Rican in a cultural scene heavily dominated by African Americans, Chase found it advantageous not to emphasize his Puerto Rican heritage; initially he employed a strategy of camouflage. During live performances he remained inconspicuous, seated toward the back of the stage, mixing his tapes and records, while the black MCs dominated the show out front. Occasionally, unknown to his crew and listeners, Chase would sneak a Latin record with a funky bass line into the mix. But rapping in Spanish, he recalls, was a rarity in the mid-1980s, especially in rhymes that were distributed on records and tapes. "A lot of people [Latinos] were doing it [rapping in Spanish] underground, but they couldn't come off doing it, they couldn't make money doing it" Chase recalls. "The people that did it, did it in parties, home stuff, the block, they were the stars in their ghetto" (Flores 1992). As rap music reached new commercial heights in the late 1980s, popular stars carefully avoided any usage of Spanish or references to anything Puerto Rican (or Latino) in their song lyrics.

Then, when "Latino rap" burst onto the scene in 1990, the whole situation changed, or so it seemed. Mellow Man Ace went gold with "Mentirosa" in the summer of that year, and Kid Frost's debut album *Hispanic Causing Panic* became the rap anthem of La Raza. Gerardo ("Rico Suave") took his place as the inevitable Latin rap sex symbol, and El General established the immense popularity of Spanish-language reggae-rap in barrios here and all over Latin

America and the Caribbean. Suddenly Spanish and the Latin sound were "in," and it was not long before high-profile performers like Queen Latifah and Nice & Smooth began sprinkling salsa and Spanglish into their recordings. The door opened in the other direction, too, as Latin groups as diverse as El Gran Combo, Wilfredo Vargas, Manny Oquendo's Libre, and Los Pleneros de la 21 let their guard down and added rap numbers to their acts. The breakthrough was so intense and so far-reaching that, by late 1991, the *Village Voice* was already referring to Latino rap as the "Next Big Thing," marking off "a defining moment in the creation of a nationwide Latino/Americano hip hop aesthetic" (Morales 1991, 91).

Such hyperbole aside, the pop emergence of bilingual rap has signalled a major opening, as the "multicultural" generalization of rap's reference and idiom finally extended to the Latino population. Rap thus goes on record as the first major style of popular music to have effected this musical and linguistic crossover, even more extensively than the Latin jazz and Latin R & B fusions of earlier generations. And coming as it did in times of loud public alarm over "America's fastest-growing minority" and a burgeoning "English-only movement," Latino rap assumes a crucial political role as well. Not only does bilingual usage become common practice in rap vocabulary, but Spanglish rhyming and the interlingual encounter have even become a theme in some of the best-known rap lyrics such as Kid Frost's "Ya Estuvo," Cypress Hill's "Funky Bi-lingo," and Latin Empire's "Palabras."

For the New York-based Puerto Ricans, for whom hip hop had long been a way of life, this victory has turned out to be Pyrrhic at best. Most obviously, none of the Latino rap superstars are Puerto Ricans from New York: Mellow Man was born in Cuba and raised in Los Angeles, Kid Frost is a Chicano from East L.A., Gerardo is from Ecuador, El General is Panamanian, and Vico C and Lisa M are Puerto Ricans from the island. What Puerto Ricans there are, even in breakthrough Latino acts like Latin Alliance, are still backgrounding their Puerto Rican identity in deference to some larger, more diluted ethnic construction. The leading Nuyorican rap group chose the name "Latin Empire" over "Rican Empire," reflecting the group's desire to situate itself in an increasingly multicultural hip hop landscape.

Yet Latin Empire clearly sees its mission as reinstating the history and geography of the New York Puerto Rican contribution to hip hop and counteracting the sensationalist version perpetrated by the media. In more recent numbers like "El Barrio," "Mi Viejo South Bronx," and "The Big Manzana" the group journeys deep into New York's Puerto Rican neighborhoods.

Tracing the transition from the gang era to the emergence of the "style wars" of hip hop, Latin Empire's members tell their own stories and dramatize their constant juggling act between black and Latino and between island and New York cultures. In a new rhyme, "Not Listed," they underscore the particular Puerto Rican role in rap history and counter the false currency given new arrivals. They end by affirming these ignored roots and rescuing the many early Puerto Rican rappers from oblivion:

> Y'all need to see a médico
> but we don't accept Medicaid
> we don't give no crédito
> we only give credit where credit is due
> we got to give it to the Mean Machine
> and the other brothers who were out there
> lookin' out for Latinos some kept it up
> some chose other caminos
> but we can't pretend that they never existed
> cause yo, they were out there, just not listed.

Latin Empire. Photo by Máximo Colón.

With all their hunger for recognition, Latin Empire also feel the burden of responsibility for being the only Nuyorican rap group given any commercial play at all. Its members realize that, being synonymous with Puerto Rican rap, they are forced to stand in for

a whole historical experience and for the rich variety of street rappers condemned to omission by the very filtering process that they
are confronting. A prime example for them of the "not listed" is the
"right hand hombre" mentioned here, MC TNT. Virtually unknown
outside the immediate hip hop community in the South Bronx, TNT
is living proof that hard-core, streetwise rhyming continues and
develops in spite of the diluting effects and choices of the managers
and A & R departments. Recently Latin Empire MC's Puerto Rock
and KT have incorporated TNT into many of their routines, and his
rhymes and delivery have added a strong sense of history and po-
etic language to their presentations.

TNT (Tomás Robles) was born in Puerto Rico and came to New
York at an early age. But childhood in the rough neighborhoods on
the island figures prominently in his raps, as in this autobiographical section interlaced with samples from Rubén Blades' "La Vida Te
Da Sorpresas":

> Este ritmo es un invento
> cuando empiezo a rimar le doy el 100 por ciento
> no me llamo Chico, o Federico
> donde naciste? Santurce, Puerto Rico
> cuando era niño no salía 'fuera
> porque mataban diario en la cantera
> esto es verdad realidad no un engaño
> mi pae murio cuando yo tenia seis años
> la muerte me afectó con mucho dolor
> pues mi mae empaquetó y nos mudamos pa' Nueva York
> cuando llegué era un ambiente diferente
> pero no me repentí, seguí para frente
> y por las noches recé a Dios y a la santa
> porque en mi corazón el coquí siempre canta.[2]

> This rhythm is an invention
> when I start to rhyme I give it 100 percent
> my name isn't Chico, or Federico
> where were you born? Santurce, Puerto Rico
> when I was a boy I didn't go outside
> because they were killing in the quarry every day
> this is true reality not a hoax
> my father died when I was six years old
> his death caused me a lot of pain
> well my mother packed up and we moved to New York
> when I arrived it was a very different atmosphere

but I didn't regret it, I moved ahead
and at night I prayed to God and the holy mother
because in my heart the *coqui* frog always sings.

At age twenty-seven (when interviewed in 1992), MC TNT was already a veteran of Spanish rap battles, still "unlisted" and waiting for his break yet still working on his rhymes and beats. His style is close to the tradition of Puerto Rican plena music, since like that of the master *pleneros* his work is taking shape as a newspaper of the barrios, a running ironic commentary on the everyday events of Puerto Rican life. When talk of referendums and plebiscites to determine the political status of Puerto Rico monopolized public discourse, TNT had some advice for his people to contemplate:

Puerto Rico, una isla hermosa
donde nacen bonitas rosas
plátanos, guineos y yautía
Sazón Goya le da sabor a la comida
y ¿quién cocina más que la tia mia?
pero el gobierno es bien armado
tratando de convertirla en un estado
es mejor la dejen libre (asociado?)
Cristobali Colón no fue nadie
cruzó el mar con un bonche de salvajes
entraron a Puerto Rico rompiendo palmas
asustando a los caciques con armas
chequéate los libros, esto es cierto
pregúntale a un cacique pero ya esta muerto
¿cómo él descubrió algo que ya está descubierto?
Boriqua, no te vendas!

Puerto Rico, a beautiful island
where there are pretty roses
plantains, bananas and root vegetables
Goya seasoning gives the food flavor
and who cooks more than my own aunt?
but the government is well armed
trying to convert it into a state
it's better to leave it free (associated?)
Christopher Columbus was nobody
he crossed the sea with a bunch of savages
they entered Puerto Rico destroying the palm trees
terrifying the Indian chiefs with their weapons

check out the books, this is true
ask one of the Indian chiefs but they're already dead
how could he discover something already discovered?
Puerto Rico, don't sell yourself!

Like other Latino peoples, Puerto Ricans are using rap as a vehicle for affirming their history, language, and culture under conditions of rampant discrimination and exclusion. The explosion of Spanish-language and bilingual rap onto the pop-music scene in recent years bears special significance in the face of the stubbornly monolingual tenor of today's public discourse, most evident in the crippling of bilingual programs and services and in the ominous gains of the English-only movement. And of course along with its Spanish and Spanglish rhymes, Latino rap carries an ensemble of alternative perspectives and an often divergent cultural ethos into the mainstream of social life in the United States. The mass diffusion, even if only for commercial purposes, of cultural expression in the "other" language, and above all its broad and warm reception by fans of all nationalities, may help to muffle the shrieks of alarm emanating from the official culture whenever mention is made of "America's fastest-growing minority." Latin rap lends volatile fuel to the cause of "multiculturalism" in our society, at least in the challenging, inclusionary sense of that embattled term.

For Puerto Ricans, though, rap is more than a newly opened window on their history; rap is their history, and Puerto Ricans are integral to the history of hip hop. As the young Puerto Rican rappers testify in conversation and rhyme, rapping is one among many social and creative practices that express their collective historical position in the prevailing relations of power and privilege. Puerto Rican participation in the emergence of hip hop music needs to be understood in direct, interactive relation to Puerto Rican experience in gangs and other forms of association among inner-city youth through the devastating blight of the 1970s. Puerto Rican hip hoppers are the children of impoverished colonial immigrants facing even tougher times than in earlier decades. They helped make rap what it was to become, just as they played a constitutive role in the stylistic definition of graffiti writing and breakdancing.

What is to become of Latino rap, and how we appreciate and understand its particular messages, will depend significantly on the continuities it forges to its roots among young Nuyoricans. Recovering this history, explicitly or by example, and "inventing" a tradition divergent from the workings of the commercial culture, represents the only hope of reversing the instant amnesia that engulfs rap and all forms of emergent cultural discourse as they migrate into the world of pop hegemony. Charlie Chase, TNT, and the other Puerto Rican rappers were pioneers not only in some nostalgic sense but helped set the social meaning of rap practice prior to and relatively independent of its mediated commercial meaning. That formative participation of Latinos in the emergence of rap is a healthy reminder that the rap attack, as David Toop argued some years ago, is but the latest outburst of "African jive," and that the age-old journey of jive has always been a motley and inclusive procession (Toop 1984). And as in Cuban-based salsa, the Puerto Rican conspiracy in the present volley shows how creatively a people can adopt and adapt what would seem a "foreign" tradition and make it, at least in part, its own. I close with a little rhyme by MC Ruby Dee (Rubén García), a snatch of poetry from the South Bronx that Machito surely would have appreciated:

> Now all you Puerto Ricans you're in for a treat,
> cause this Puerto Rican can rock a funky beat.
> If you fall on your butt and you start to bleed,
> Ruby Dee is what all the Puerto Ricans need.
> I'm a homeboy to them cause I know what to do,
> cause Ruby Dee is down with the black people too.

NOTES

1. Portions of the first half of this article are taken from the author's initial publication on Puerto Rican hip hop culture (Flores 1987). Portions of the second half are taken from more recent writings on Latin rap music (Flores 1994; Flores 1996).

2. Lyrics to TNT's raps were recorded during a personal interview with the author in July, 1992.

REFERENCES CITED

Castleman, Craig. 1982. *Getting Up: Subway Graffiti in New York*. Cambridge: MIT Press.

Colón, Jesús. 1961. *A Puerto Rican in New York*. New York: International Press.

Flores, Juan. 1987. "Rappin', Writin' and Breakin': Black and Puerto Rican Street Culture in New York City." *Dissent* (Fall): 580-584.

_____. 1992. "It's a Street Thing!" *Callaloo* 4 (Fall): 999-1021.

_____.1994. "Puerto Rican and Proud, Boyee!: Rap, Roots and Amnesia." In *Microphone Fiends: Youth Music and Youth Culture*, ed. Andrew Ross and Tricia Rose, 89-98. New York: Routledge.

_____. 1996. "Puerto Rocks: New York Ricans State Their Claim." In *Droppin' Science: Critical Essays on Rap Music and Hip Hop Culture*, ed. William Eric Perkins, 85-105. Philadelphia: Temple University Press.

Hager, Steven. 1984. *Hip Hop: The Illustrated History of Break Dancing, Rap Music, and Graffiti*. New York: St. Martin's Press.

Mailer, Norman. 1974. "The Faith of Graffiti." *Esquire*.

Morales, Ed. 1991. "How Ya Like Nosotros Now?" *Village Voice* (26 November): 91.

Roberts, John Storm. 1979. *The Latin Tinge: The Impact of Latin American Music on the United States*. New York: Oxford University Press.

Salazar, Max. 1992. "Afro-American Latinized Rhythms." In *Salsiology: Afro-Cuban Music and the Evolution of Salsa in New York City*, ed. Vernon Boggs, 239-248. New York: Excelsior Music Publishing Company.

Thomas, Piri. 1967. *Down These Mean Streets*. New York: Alfred A. Knopf.

Toop, David. 1984. *The Rap Attack: African Jive to New York Hip Hop*. London: South End Press.

Vázquez, Denis. April 1983. Personal conversation with author.

"I Am Happy Just to Be in This Sweet Land of Liberty"
The New York City Calypso Craze of the 1930s and 1940s

Donald Hill

American music devotees of the post-World War Two generation know calypso as a style of West Indian music that was popular in the 1950s. The name Harry Belafonte comes immediately to mind, for he, along with a host of other North Americans, popularized the style in the United States. But older aficionados may recall calypso as a popular style that flourished in New York in the late 1930s and 1940s. During this period Trinidadian calypsonians played in Manhattan clubs, cut records aimed at a North American clientele, and appeared on local, national, and international radio broadcasts. This first calypso boom in the United States lasted roughly from 1935 to 1947, when a generation of New York-based West Indians developed calypsos that began to differ from their Trinidadian counterparts. This essay will focus on this initial calypso craze, exploring how Trinidadian calypso became part of the fabric of North American popular music, reaching a diverse audience of white and black New Yorkers as well as West Indian listeners.

The roots of West Indian calypso stretch back to the Carnival celebrations of Trinidad. There African-style call-and-response singing, accompanied by dense percussion, became an integral part of late nineteenth-century Carnival activities. By the turn of the twentieth century more lyrical, textually oriented calypsos began to evolve in Carnival arenas known as tents. These tent calypsos, characterized by witty satire and biting social commentary, were eventually carried north by Trinidadian emigrants bound for New York City (Hill 1993, 64-114).

Early Recording of Calypso for the West Indian Market

Throughout the early decades of this century New York City's West Indian community remained culturally distinct from its African-American neighbors (Watkins-Owens 1996; Lewis 1981), but relatively small in size.[1] Not surprisingly, most of the calypsos recorded in New York from the 1910s through the mid-1930s were not marketed to the city's West Indian immigrants, but exported back to Trinidad and South America.[2] As early as 1912 George Bailey (a.k.a. "Lovey") brought his band from Trinidad to New York to record West Indian songs for the people back home. Lionel Belasco followed, recording as a piano soloist and with his band. In the late 1920s Wilmoth Houdini, touted as the "Calypso King of New York," recorded with Belasco's orchestra and emerged as the dominant West Indian vocalist. West Indians Sam Manning, Walter Merrick, Johnny Walker, and Phil Madison also recorded during this period.

Until the late 1930s only a few recordings mention New York or North American themes. Sam Manning's 1928 recording "West Indian Man and American Woman" was especially interesting, and clearly marketed to both African Americans and West Indians because it played to the stereotypes each had of the other. Manning, a Trinidadian who was really more of a stage performer than a calypsonian, did appeal to both West Indian immigrants in New York and to black Americans, and often performed in Harlem stage reviews. But other singers and musicians recorded few songs in this vein. For the most part, calypso recordings in New York concerned life in Trinidad. The calypsos recorded by Houdini, Walter Merrick, Belasco, and Cyril Monrose, with their old fashioned Venezuelan-style string band accompaniments (popular in Trinidad since the 1890s), are a marvelous document of early twentieth-century Trinidadian Carnival music.[3] Their songs, however, had little appeal to North Americans.

Calypso for North American Audiences

During the early years of the Depression few West Indians immigrated to the United States; rather it is likely that many returned home. But the resumption of economic activity spurred a second phase of West Indian immigration to the United States that began in the late 1930s and lasted through the mid-1960s, when immigration laws changed (Kasinitz 1992, 24).[4] Around 1935, just prior to this second wave of immigration, calypsonians turned their attention to North American topics, and the New York calypso boom was underway.

In Trinidad, Carnival was the driving force behind calypso and the music remained close to its folk roots. But in New York City, recordings, radio performances, and club appearances worked together to spread the popularity of new calypsos which exhibited few connections to Trinidadian Carnival. Even those calypsos that may have originated in Carnival tents took on lives of their own once they reached New York, thus signaling a fundamental change in the nature of calypso outside Trinidad, as the music evolved into a form of popular entertainment aimed primarily at North American listeners.

In 1934 Gerald Clark, a Trinidadian guitar and cuatro player who had originally immigrated to the United States intent on attending medical school, formed a band called the Caribbean Serenaders. The ensemble soon hosted a Sunday afternoon radio show on radio WHN in New York. "The chief appeal of the Caribbean Serenaders directed by Gerald Clark is that they're different" wrote a reviewer for *Variety*, 13 February 1934. Prophetically, the observer went on to state: "the band belongs in a class drinking restaurant, if not already thus engaged." Calypso was poised to move into a broader arena.

Later in 1934 Decca and the American Recording Company (ARC) brought fresh talent from Trinidad to record in New York City. The Roaring Lion (Rafael De Leon) and Atilla the Hun (Raymond Quevedo) headed the new wave of calypsonians. Tiger (Neville Marcano), Beginner (Egbert Moore), Executor (Philip Garcia), Caresser (Rufus Callender), Invader (Rupert Grant), and others followed throughout the 1930s. According to Hollis Liverpool it was a great thrill for these singers to come to the United States,[5] the "sweet land of liberty," as the country is called in a calypso recorded by the Duke of Iron (Cecil Anderson) with Gerald Clark's orchestra:

I am happy just to be,
in this sweet land of liberty.
Standards of living here,
is much higher than anywhere.
With Mr. Roosevelt at the head,
American people bound to eat bread.
For who pays the rent when you ain't got a cent?
And who gets you meat when you have none to eat?
Now where can you roam when you ain't got a home?
Oh where can you flee to a land that is free?
USA![6]

Lion and Atilla gained status when they returned home and told countrymen of their encounters with the entertainer Rudy Vallee and even with President Roosevelt. "Up to this very day," Hollis Liverpool continues, "you ask Lion about it, he will tell you that the major thrill in his career was [the] coast-to-coast radio [broadcast] singing with Rudy Vallee on stage." Lion and Atilla sang of their encounter with Rudy Vallee, tenor singer and orchestra leader, in a 1938 recording:

> We were making records for the Decca Company,
> when we were heard by Rudy Vallee.
> Well he was so charmed with our rhythmic harmony,
> he took us in hand immediately.
> "You boys are wonderful," by Rudy Vallee we were told.
> "You must throw your voice to the whole wide world."
> And so you should a see the Lion and me,
> with Mae West and Rudy Vallee.[7]

Bing Crosby and Rudy Vallee joined the calypsonians in the studio for some of their early New York recordings.

The Trinidadian singers who came to record in New York City in the mid-1930s began to write and perform a few calypsos focusing on North American, rather than Trinidadian, subject matter. Popular recordings paid homage to American singers like the Four Mills Brothers, praised the great African-American boxer Joe Louis, bemoaned the kidnapping of the Lindbergh baby, and warned of Hitler's danger to the world. These new calypsos reflected the Trinidadian singers' growing interest in the life and culture of the United States, as well as their desire to reach a broader, non-West Indian audience.

The number of recordings recounting the exploits of boxer Joe Louis reveal the deep admiration West Indians held for the black American legend. In one rendition recorded near the end of the great boxer's career, Lord Beginner intones:

> The Brown Bomber as the world's renowned,
> really defended his crown.
> He won the people of every place,
> he made a name for the colored race.
> He represented his country,
> faithfully and fearlessly.
> He even joined the army,
> and gave them money generously.[8]

By far the most influential recordings made in 1937 were Caresser's "Edward VIII" and Atilla's "Roosevelt in Trinidad." The former song chronicles King Edward VIII's 1936 abdication from the throne of Britain in order to marry a North American divorcée, Wallis Simpson:

chorus:
It's love, love alone,
that caused King Edward to leave the throne.

We know Edward is noble and great,
but love caused him to abdicate.
Oh, what a sad disappointment,
was endured by the British government.
On the tenth of December *[sic]* we heard a talk,
that he gave the throne to the Duke of York.
"I'm sorry my mother is going to grieve,
but I cannot help, I'm bound to leave."
Lord Baldwin tried to break down his plan,
he said, "Come what may," the American.
We got the money, we got the talk,
and the fancy walk just to suit New York.
"And if I can't get a boat to set me free,
well, I'll walk to Miss Simpson across the sea."
He said, "My robes and my crown is upon my mind,
but I cannot leave Miss Simpson behind.
They could take my throne, they could take my crown,
but leave me and Miss Simpson alone."
Let the organ roll, let the church bell ring,
good luck to our second bachelor king.[9]

Atilla's "Roosevelt in Trinidad," commenting on the famous American president's visit, sold well and did much to popularize calypso among white audiences in New York and elsewhere in the United States.

When Roosevelt came to the Land of the Hummingbird,
shouts of welcome were heard.
His visit to the island is bound to be,
an epoch in local history.
Definitely marking the new era,
between Trinidad and America.[10]

Amidst all this recording activity calypsonians, especially Houdini, continued to perform in New York for West Indian and African-American audiences. But by the late 1930s West Indian bands like Gerald Clark's Caribbean Serenaders were playing uptown venues (the Apollo Theater), midtown dance halls (the Hotel Seville and the Renaissance Ballroom), and Greenwich Village nightspots (the Village Vanguard). This latter "downtown" scene proved especially important, for a new calypso audience of primarily middle-class, white listeners was developing in Greenwich Village. This trend parallels, in a much smaller way, what was happening in Latin American music beginning in the late 1920s. For example, Ruth Glasser (1995, 112-28) contrasts the performance environments in the communities where Puerto Ricans and other Latinos lived, generally in uptown Manhattan, with the non-Latino, predominantly white venues located in midtown and lower Manhattan. While musicians liked to perform for their own people, most preferred the better money to be found in the white clubs. A complex relationship developed between trends set in one location and then picked up in another.

The Greenwich Village Scene

In the summer of 1939 in the Village Vanguard cafe, a small theater group called "The Revuers" had just closed, to reopen in September at the more luxurious Rainbow Room in midtown. According to Richard Manson of the *New York Post*, 26 August 1939, Vanguard owner Max Gordon replaced the theater troupe with an unknown group that called itself the Calypso Recorders. Gordon hired the Trinidadian singers after hearing one of their records that a customer had accidentally left at the club. He later commented to Malcolm Johnson of the *New York Sun*, 5 April 1940:

> The music was unusual and the ballad, based on the romance of King Edward VIII and Mrs. Simpson, was delightfully satirical, I thought. It would be something new in night club entertainment. With this in mind I got in touch with these players and immediately signed them for the Vanguard. They worked here for ten weeks, during which time my business more than doubled. Enthusiasts who had heard their records flocked to hear them in person.

The biggest catalyst to the New York calypso boom was the engagement of Gerald Clark and his Caribbean Serenaders at the Vanguard in 1939. Clark headed the ensemble and hired the calypso

singers and West Indian dancers for the floor show. Several calypso
tent singers, particularly Caresser and Invader, gained fame for the
first time outside of Trinidad by singing with Clark at the Vanguard.
Others, although born in Trinidad, had no extensive background in
the calypso tents. These singers, including the Duke of Iron, MacBeth
the Great, and Sir Lancelot, took advantage of calypso's growing
popularity at the Vanguard and other New York venues to launch
their careers.

*Calypso singers (left to right) Invader, Radio, Atilla, and Tiger in costume at
the Village Vanguard, 1949. Photo courtesy of Donald Hill.*

The large metropolitan dailies reported the doings at the Vanguard as the calypsonians, especially the New York-based singers,
began creating songs for North American audiences. The previously
mentioned "Roosevelt in Trinidad" and "Edward VIII" were big sell-
ers outside of Trinidad, and brought whites to the Vanguard to hear
the new calypso in person:

> Catering to the younger set of Greenwich Village, those who
> seek "atmosphere" in that section and, all in all, a politically
> well-informed group, Max Gordon, after successfully bringing
> to the fore the Vanguard (Calypso) Players, is again featuring a
> unique floor show.

Starring the Calypso Kid, dancers and Gerald Clark and his Caribbean Serenaders, the show is entertaining and different. It is exactly what the Vanguard patrons want. While the show seeks to depict the change in the Village, the calypso group reflects the time when the club was the Bohemian hangout for poets and writers. The show runs 40 minutes.[11]

Caresser's "Edward the VIII," Atilla's "Roosevelt in Trinidad," and other topical songs were made into small skits, as was sometimes done in Trinidad. Both the singers and non-singing West Indian entertainers played various parts in costume. The hit recordings were sung by Macbeth, Lancelot, or the Duke of Iron:

Knowing that his audience understands the political situation Bill Matons, the "Calypso Kid," who also stages the revue, has brought prominent political issues and events to the front in each act. The first "King Edward and Wally" shows, in pantomime and dance, Edward's problem choosing between the crown and the "woman he loves," Wallis Simpson. "President Roosevelt in Trinidad," with Matons as FDR, shows the great admiration these people hold for the Chief Executive...The "Duke of Iron" (Cecil Anderson) handles the narration.[12]

As Gerald Clark was beginning his second successful run at the Village Vanguard in 1940, he made several recordings for the Varsity label with the singers he had engaged at the club. The most interesting of these were "Walter Winchell," "USA," "Camilla the Jitterbug," "G Man Hoover," and "I Love to Read Magazines."[13] A reviewer for *New York American*, 7 January 1940, enthusiastically reported:

A couple of orchids to Gerald Clark, the "Duke of Iron," and his Calypso Orchestra, for "Walter Winchell," a hilarious biography of the columnist from Gus Edwards days [a vaudeville impresario who gave the influential gossip columnist his first job] to the present, including a couple of "flashes" [Winchell's trademark telegraph-like sound that opened each broadcast].

Recorded in 1939, the text of "Walter Winchell" begins:

It was in nineteen hundred and eight,
that Edwards put Walter on the stage.
He soon became a vaudeville star,

young Winchell was famous near and far.
But now he sings through the daily press,
and gets the scandals 'fore they confess.
They say the dirt that he get upon the Great White Way,
enough to bury him whenever he should die.

Flash! Duck your head, hide yourself,
Walter Winchell' peeping at you.
(chorus:) Through the keyhole.

Flash! Pull the shades when you bathe,
Walter Winchell' peeping at you.
(chorus:) Exclusive!
Flash! Duck your head, hide yourself,
Walter Winchell' peeping at you.
(chorus:) Through the key hole.
Flash! Pull the shades when you bathe,
Walter Winchell's peeping at you.[14]

Winchell was the country's leading gossip columnist in the late 1930s, before his left-wing political leanings took a hard right turn. To satirize a man who could make or break entertainers was a risky thing to do, but fortunately for the Duke of Iron and the Varsity label Winchell and other media critics apparently liked the song. Advertisers claimed that "Walter Winchell" and other Varsity calypso recordings were well suited for North American ears. One Varsity advertisement in a mainstream New York publication proclaimed "The best calypso enunciation on the market!"[15]

In early January of 1940 Gerald Clark, Lancelot, the Duke of Iron, Macbeth, and others began their second engagement at the Village Vanguard which, after being extended, lasted through the summer. This time Gerald Clark was prepared to make Trinidadian English more understandable to his New Yorker audience, as Malcolm Johnson noted in the *New York Sun*, 24 May 1940:

> ...Gerald Clark and his Calypso Singers, currently holding forth at the Village Vanguard, are preparing a calypso glossary to consist of the racy French jargon and English idioms frequently employed in the ballads with their American translations—all for the benefit of their patrons. The glossary is being done up on mimeographed sheets, with the words and their translations under the songs in which they are found.

Lengthy appearances at Café Society, Le Ruban Bleu, and especially the Village Vanguard put calypso on the map of bohemian New Yorkers, the smart set of Manhattan. Walter Winchell, Malcolm Johnson, and other mainstream columnists, as well as writers for the leftist *Daily Worker* and *PM Magazine*, brought considerable attention to the growing club scene. In Greenwich Village, as in Trinidad, calypso functioned to explain the great social issues of the day, as well as the doings of the club patrons. Songs about Walter Winchell, President Roosevelt, Bing Crosby, Mae West and Joe Louis shared billing with texts about poverty, politics, and the distant thunder of the European war.

Decca and Houdini Court the North American Audience

The first album of 78 RPM recordings of calypsos came out in 1939, during Gerald Clark's initial engagement at the Village Vanguard. Entitled *Decca Presents a Special Collection of the World-Famous Music of Trinidad*, it featured the old master, Houdini, accompanied by His Royal Calypso Orchestra. Wilmoth Fredericks, better known as "Houdini," had performed in both Carnival masquerades and in tents in the exuberant 1919 Trinidad Carnival that followed the close of World War I. In the late 1920s, after a brief stint as a seaman, he settled in Harlem and began recording with Lionel Belasco's orchestra. From 1928 until 1934 he was the most prominent calypsonian recording in New York.

Even after he had established his principal base in New York, Houdini kept contact with his Trinidadian sources. He occasionally returned to the island during Carnival season for new material to record. "Of course, I have to go back to Trinidad to renew me inspiration," he later told writer Joseph Mitchell of the *New Yorker*, 6 May 1939. This "inspiration" often consisted of other calypsonians' compositions. According to Hollis Liverpool:

> His name tells you something about him. Houdini [is] a kind of magician; he "borrowed" a lot of the melodies from the calypsonians in Trinidad. He was able to come up here [to New York and] take the melodies and apply them to many of his songs. And Beginner will tell you that Houdini was a thief, that he stole all the melodies [and] lyrics. But who was there to tell him that he was wrong? Who has the right to tell him that he shouldn't do these things?[16]

Wilmoth "Houdini" Fredericks in Carnival costume, circa 1939.
Photo courtesy of Donald Hill.

Houdini's album was Decca's attempt to get at this new, booming calypso market of North Americans. As an album, it was issued in a popular series aimed at the broadest possible market in the United States. Decca boxed three 78 RPM records together as an "album" set. "The Welcome of Their Majesties" on Decca 18006 was a song about the visit of British royalty to the New York World's Fair, a venue that Houdini played. The other side of that record was "Hot Dogs Made Their Name," a song with classic double entendre. "Johnny Take My Wife," Decca 18007, was one of Houdini's old favorites about a domestic dispute. The other side was "Roosevelt Opens The World's Fair." The last record, Decca 18005, featured "Monkey Swing" and "He Had It Coming" (also known as "Stone Cold Dead in the Market"), a song Houdini had copyrighted, although it was, in fact, a Barbadian folk song about a marketplace killing. The song was recorded several years later by the popular African-American artists Louis Jordan and Ella Fitzgerald.

Decca issued a second album of 78 RPM records by Houdini and His Royal Calypso Orchestra, entitled *Harlem Seen Through Calypso Eyes*. Recorded in September of 1940, the collection was tailor made for the North American market. It was the first concept album of calypsos in that all the songs used Harlem as their theme: "Harlem Alley Cat," "Married Life in Harlem," "The Million Dollar Pair of Feet" (a song about famed black American dancer and actor Bill "Bojangles" Robinson), "Good Old Harlem Town," "Harlem Popcorn Man," and "Harlem Night Life." This last song, based on an old double-entendre calypso "Dingolay" and the Spiritual Baptist hymn "Glory Day," captures the flavor of a West Indian attending a Harlem rent party. The song's protagonist marvels at the African-American food and dance, but bemoans the lack of West Indian music:

I went to a Harlem house rent party,
everybody was gay and happy.
At this Harlem house rent party,
everybody was gay and happy.
The guests were showing what they can do,
dancing rumba and boogie too.
But one tune they forgot to play,
is a West Indian song we call "Dingolay."

I went to a Harlem house rent party,
King Kong liquor was flowing free.
I went to a Harlem house rent party,
King Kong liquor was flowing free.
They served pigs feet and tater salad,
chitlins patties and fried chicken.
But the one tune they forgot to play,
is a West Indian song we call "Glory Day."[17]

In April of 1941 Decca issued another 78 RPM album recorded in New York, entitled *Decca Presents Topical Songs From the West Indian Island of Trinidad*. Featuring Gerald Clark's orchestra and calypsonians Atilla, Radio, Destroyer, and Lion, the album was the first to market authentic, Carnival-tested calypsonians to the general North American audience. The titles included Lion's "Bing Crosby" and "Ugly Woman," probably the most popular songs in the set. Also included were "Roosevelt's Election" and the "Red Cross Society" by Atilla, and "Jitterbug" by Radio.

The last Decca calypso album recorded before World War II was Sam Manning's *West Indian Folk Songs*. All Manning's sides were recorded on December 5, 1941, just two days before the Japanese attack on the United States naval base at Pearl Harbor. Unfortunately the album did not sell well, although it was marketed for a general audience. Record sales declined drastically in the years that followed, due to war shortages and the devastating effects of the 1942 American Federation of Musicians' recording strike. Then, in the fall of 1943, following the settlement of the musicians' recording strike, Decca released what would prove to be its biggest calypso hit to date. Ironically the singers were not Trinidadian, but rather a popular American female trio, the Andrews Sisters.

"Rum and Coca-Cola" and the Post-War Years

In the early 1940s, Lord Invader (Rupert Grant), one of Trinidad's foremost calypsonians, popularized a modified version of an old Martiniquean folk song under the title "Rum and Coca-Cola." The song eventually found its way to the United States—probably through the efforts of American entertainer Morey Amsterdam—where it was published by Leo Feist Inc. and recorded by the Andrews Sisters for Decca.[18]

The Andrews Sisters' version of "Rum and Coca-Cola" was the most successful calypso crossover by non-Trinidadian singers, foreshadowing a trend that would bring national notoriety to calypso in the 1950s. For Decca, the Andrews Sisters' recording helped launch the label ahead of its rivals after they settled with the American Federation of Musicians. Four million copies of the record were sold in 1946 alone (Brown 1947, 52), helping to lift Decca, and the record industry in general, past the musicians' recording strike and through the war years. The song introduced millions of North American listeners to calypso, or at least a popular interpretation of calypso. By the early post-war years calypso's popularity was spreading across the United States:

> Juke boxes account for a large proportion of the sales of calypso records sold in America, for you'll find at least one of the Trinidadian records in almost any of the 450,000 juke boxes scattered over the States. While "Rum and Coca-Cola" has a big lead in popularity, other calypsos such as "Ugly Woman," "Donkey City," and "Bum-Bum-Bum" have sold around the million mark. Two Manhattan night clubs have calypsonians as regular features of their program. These are the Caribbean Club in Harlem run by two Trinidadian brothers, Boxil and Wycliffe Jackson, and the Vanguard in Greenwich Village. Harlem theaters, too, specialize in calypso, and the Duke of Iron was a long-time favorite at the famous Apollo Theater on 125th Street (Brown 1947, 52-53).

After World War Two new calypso recordings kept up a steady

pace as the nature of the market changed. North Americans, black and white, were interested in the genre as a popular style. What had been separate black and white American audiences fused into one big calypso market. Decca recorded Houdini twice in 1945, including a best selling, two-sided version of "Rum and Coca-Cola" (Cowley 1993). In the Spring of 1945 Decca also recorded eight selections each by Lord Invader, Beginner, Tiger, and Radio, all accompanied by Lionel Belasco's orchestra. Decca made no additional 78 RPM recordings in the United States as smaller, primarily New York-based companies like Disc, Guild, Keynote, Continental, and Apollo took over the market. Later, Folkways and other labels would cut LPs with Invader, the Duke of Iron, and others.

In 1946 the Disc label released an album with the simple title *Calypso*. The recording spotlighted Lord Invader and Lord Beginner accompanied by Felix and His Internationals, rather than Gerald Clark, who usually accompanied the calypsonians in the United States. The album art was drawn by David Stone Martin, who would soon be famous for his sketches and his album covers of jazz musicians. *Calypso* featured the classic "New York Subway" by Invader:

> When I first landed in the U.S.A.,
> listen how I got lost on the subway.
> I had a date with a chick and I went to Brooklyn,
> but I couldn't find my way back the following morning.
> I had money yet I had to roam,
> and still I couldn't get a cab to drop me back home.
>
> I met a cop and told him I'm a stranger,
> Lord Invader a calypso singer.
> I live in Harlem and came here yesterday,
> But now I want to go home I can't find my way.
> He told me, "Walk back three blocks" and he further explain,
> "Go to the subway and take the uptown train."
> I got confused, I was in a heat,
> I couldn't find my way to One-Twenty-Fifth Street.
>
> I came out the subway and didn't know what to do,
> looking for someone to help me through.
> You talk about people as bad as crab,
> is the drivers who driving the taxicab.
> Some passing you empty and yet they wouldn't stop,
> some will say they have no gas or they can't make the drop.
> I had money yet I had to roam,
> but still I couldn't get a cab to drop me back home.

I console myself and started to walk,
I said that happen to persons who born in New York.
So I decided to leave the girls alone,
if they want to see me they must come to my home.
Because New York is so big it take a year and a day,
for anyone to get accustom to the subway.
I had money yet I had to roam,
and still I couldn't get a cab to drop me back home.[19]

The song recounts not only the vicissitudes of New York subway travel, but also the insulting racial discrimination that West Indians, as Blacks, experienced on a daily basis. Hollis Liverpool explains the song:

> [The calypsonians] were bringing back to Trinidad and to the Caribbean some of their experiences; so the song about the subway and the cab [mentions things that home-based Trinidadians] had never seen. I myself was lost on the subway when I came here in 1965! Sometimes we hide things in calypso; [there are] little masks in the calypso. The masks hide the fact that [Invader had] money and [yet] he couldn't go home. And the taxi drivers simply would not pick him up. So the end of each [verse] in [the] calypso ends with, 'I couldn't get that car to drive me or to drop me back home.' So obviously he was speaking of the prejudices he experienced when he came here in the 40s.[20]

Another notable recording, released in the late 1940s by the Apollo label, was entitled *Apollo Presents Calypso by King Houdini and His Calypso Parliament*. Many of its songs focused on North American topics, including "Bobby Sox Idol" (about Frank Sinatra), "Gravel Gertie" (a comic strip character), "Brave Son of America" (General Douglas MacArthur), "New Orleans Woman," and "Queen of the Amazon" (Brazilian singer and film star Carmen Miranda). In the last example Houdini sings, "She has the prettiest white skin that you've ever seen," but in one of the alternate takes he sings, "She has the prettiest brown skin that you have ever seen." The alternate line would appeal to Trinidadian listeners, while the line that was issued was probably meant for white, North American audiences.

By the time Lion appeared at the Village Vanguard in 1945, interest in calypso was firmly established in New York. In 1946 calypso gained even more favorable recognition with shows at Carnegie Hall, the New York venue that signifies recognition. A 3 May 1947 announcement in the *New York Amsterdam News* reported a gala program headlining Wilmoth Houdini, Lord Invader, and the Great Macbeth backed by Lionel "Babu" Belasco and His Orchestra, and also featuring Princess Orelia and Her Native Dancers. Then, on 28 November 1947, calypso hit Broadway, as the *New York Amsterdam News* reported the following day:

> Broadway will see its first All-Calypso musical revue when "Caribbean Carnival," a big singing and dancing show opens Friday, November 28, at the International Theater.
>
> With such headliners as Pearl Primus and Josephine Premice, the revue has a score written by Adolph Thenstead and Samuel Manning who also serve as producer and director, respectively. Thenstead and Manning have previously written a number of song hits that have served to further the popularity of Calypso music in this country...
>
> Other featured players include Claude Marchant, remembered from 'Cabin in the Sky' and 'Show Boat'; the Duke of Iron, foremost Calypso singer; the Smith Kids, Peggy Watson, the Trio Cubana, and Gregory Felix and the Caribbean Calypso Band. The supporting cast includes a chorus of fifty singers and dancers.

By the late 1940s calypso was, on the one hand, folding into a broadly Caribbean culture in the United States, while on the other it was about to become a popular style of music performed by North Americans as well. Harry Belafonte, born in New York of Jamaican parentage, gained fame in the United States in the 1950s singing popular calypsos and West Indian folk songs. African-American popular vocalists like Louis Jordan, and white American folk revival groups like the Kingston Trio and the Limelighters, included popular calypsos in their repertoires. In the 1950s their singles and albums would far outsell anything made by Trinidadian calypsonians. Through the efforts of Belafonte and other American singers, calypso in the United States became more or less independent from its Trinidadian parent, although Trinidadians continued to perform in the United States and Belafonte continued to add authentic calypsos to his song bag. For a very brief period in the 1950s this North American "folk" calypso was nearly as popular as rock 'n' roll. But North American calypso soon went the way of all fads and vanished, only to emerge again in a refreshed West Indian form in the late 1960s, on the heels of a third wave of West Indian immigration.

NOTES

1. The first wave of English-speaking Caribbean immigrants came to the United States between 1900 and 1920, many arriving during and shortly after World War One (Kasinitz 1992, 19-37). A total of 33,012 foreign Blacks immigrated to the United States between 1920 and 1930 (Hall 1935, 21). It is not possible to determine exactly how many of these immigrants were Trinidadians, as the census then had a catchall category called "foreign born" Blacks, which was only slightly larger than the sum of the English-speaking and Haitian immigration (Kasinitz 1992, 24fn). By 1930 approximately 178,000 foreign born Blacks and their children lived in the United States (Kasinitz 1992, 24), and about sixty percent of these lived in New York (Hall 1935, 17).

2. Many of the instrumental dance records cut by Lionel Belasco appeared in Spanish language catalogs marketed to Venezuela and other South American countries.

3. These early West Indian recordings featured a variety of authentic Trinidadian Carnival songs and instrumental pieces, many originally from oral tradition. Included were *leggos* (fast tunes meant for the streets on Carnival Tuesday); the so-called "single tone" and "double tone" calypsos (tunes with one or two melodies, respectively, the latter comprising one section sung in "speech tones" and another in call-and-response); popular dances such as the *castillian*; and *kalindas* (sung for stick fighting competitions).

4. Kasinitz's third phase of West Indian immigration to the United States begins in 1965 and is beyond the scope of this paper.

5. Hollis Liverpool's comments throughout this paper were made on 29 April 1995, during the "Island Sounds in the Global City" conference on Caribbean music in New York City held at Brooklyn College.

6. "USA," Varsity 8183, recorded by the Duke of Iron in New York City, 1939.

7. "Guest of Rudy Vallee," Decca 17389, recorded by the Lion and Atilla the Hun with the Cyril Monrose String Orchestra in Trinidad, 1938.

8. "The Joe Louis Calypso," Melodisc 1131, recorded by Lord Beginner and the Calypso Kings in New York City, 1952.

9. "Edward VIII," Decca 17298, recorded by Caresser in New York City, 1937.

10. "Roosevelt in Trinidad," Decca 17302, recorded by Atilla the Hun in New York City, 1937.

11. This reference is from an article found in Gerald Clark's scrapbook (n.d.). It included no bibliographic particulars, but was probably from the *Daily Worker*, the Communist newspaper printed in New York, which reported on Clark's orchestra with some regularity.

12. Ibid.

13. "Walter Winchell" was released on Varsity 8130 and "USA" on Varsity 8138. "Camilla the Jitterbug" and "G Man Hoover" were released on Varsity 8188. "I Love to Read Magazines" was released on Varsity 8195.

14. "Walter Winchell," Varsity 8130, recorded by Gerald Clark and the Duke of Iron in New York City, 1939.

15. Advertisement for Varsity records in Gerald Clark's scrapbook, n.d. (copy in author's files).

16. Hollis Liverpool, op. cit.

17. "Harlem Night Life," Decca 18102, recorded by Houdini in New York City, 1940.

18. The Andrews Sisters' recording of "Rum and Coca-Cola" instigated the most important song plagiarism suit of its day. Lord Invader was not credited as composer or arranger by publisher Leo Feist, nor by Decca Records on the Andrews Sisters' recording. Accordingly he received no royalties. After a series of legal battles Invader finally won a settlement in 1950 and was awarded $100,000 in back royalties (see Hill 1993, 234-237; Cowley 1993).

19. "New York Subway," Disc 5009, recorded by Lord Invader in New York City, 1946.

20. Hollis Liverpool, op. cit.

REFERENCES CITED

Abel. 1934. *Variety.* (Feb. 13).

Brown, Wenzell. 1947. "How Calypso Was Born." *Negro Digest* (June).

Carr, Andrew. ND. "Conversations with Calypsonians of the Past." Unpublished manuscript edited and annotated by Donald R. Hill.

Cowley, John. 1993. "L'Annee Passee: Selected Repertoire in English-speaking West Indian Music 1900-1960." *Keskidee Journal* (No. 3, Summer).

_____. ND. "West Indian Blues, A Historical Overview." Unpublished manuscript.

Glasser, Ruth. 1995. *My Music is My Flag: Puerto Rican Musicians and Their New York Communities, 1917-1940.* Berkeley: University of California Press.

Hall, Charles E. 1935. *Negroes in the United States 1920-32.* Washington: Government Printing Office.

Hill, Donald R. *Calypso Calaloo.* 1993. Gainesville: University of Florida Press.

Kasinitz, Philip. 1992. *Caribbean New York: Black Immigrants and the Politics of Race.* Ithaca: Cornell University Press.

Lewis, David. 1981. *When Harlem Is in Vogue.* New York: Alfred A. Knopf.

Watkins-Owens, Irma. 1996. *Blood Relations: Caribbean Immigrants and the Harlem Community, 1900-1930.* Bloomington: Indiana University Press.

Community Dramatized, Community Contested
The Politics of Celebration in the Brooklyn Carnival[1]

Philip Kasinitz

> Carnival does not know footlights, in the sense that it does not
> acknowledge any distinction between actors and spectators.
> Footlights would destroy a Carnival, as the absence of footlights
> would destroy a theatrical performance.
>
> Mikhail Bakhtin (1968, 7)

Most of the contributors to the present volume are ethnomusicologists, folklorists, and cultural critics. I envy them. As a sociologist and student of international migration, I have spent a good
deal of time over the years explaining to my colleagues why I think
public celebrations, and particularly Brooklyn's Labor Day Carnival, have important lessons to teach us about the social structure of
an increasingly global city. Our close cousins the anthropologists
and the social historians have generally been more sympathetic to
the idea that the cultural products and celebratory events of ordinary people can not only be a window on to their lives, but also an
arena of critique and challenge to the conditions that shape those
lives. As the late Frank Manning wrote in 1984:

> Celebration does not resolve or remove ambiguity and con-
> flict, but rather it embellishes them. It locates these social
> facts...in a performance context in which they can be thought
> about, acted upon and aesthetically appreciated. The cele-
> brants' hope...is that the rhythm of performance will find an
> echo in life, if only for the moment.

Such public events are often the arenas in which shifting social identities are both crystallized and transformed. Nowhere is this more true than in the ethnic celebrations that punctuate the annual calendars of multiethnic cities like New York. Yet with a few notable exceptions sociologists have turned a tin ear toward the social significance of such celebrations. Several years ago, not long after I began studying Brooklyn's Labor Day Carnival, I gave a talk at a sociology department of a leading university. When the time for questions came, a prominent senior colleague, clearly somewhat miffed that I had taken up an hour of his valuable time with such trivia, asked, "But isn't this just a bunch of poor people dancing around and getting drunk?"

Long ignored by the rest of the city, Brooklyn's Labor Day Carnival is indeed a celebration by people, many poor, many not, in which many do dance and more than a few do get drunk! Yet there is also something serious going on. Next to the stilt walkers and the fantastic dragon, signs with commentary about United States and Caribbean politics sometimes appear. A band of masqueraders in elaborate "African" garb is accompanied by slogans about black pride and the liberation of Nelson Mandela. And the year the Duvaliers were overthrown, the old blue and red flag of pre-Papa Doc Haiti waved above some of the most uninhibited of the dancers.

Local politicians, always the first to sense a shift in the political climate, started to come to Carnival in the early 1980s. As the decade went on, national political figures began to add Brooklyn to their Labor Day itineraries. Then, in 1991, the eyes of the nation were focused on Crown Heights as Carnival followed closely on the heels of racial disturbances. Since that time the event has become the annual occasion for the New York press to assess the state of the West Indian community, now the largest immigrant group in this city of immigrants. Today the Labor Day procession is a defining moment in the political and cultural life of Caribbean New York. Both its location and schedule are considered inviolable.

Held annually since 1969 in Brooklyn's Crown Heights, Carnival brings together more than a million people from New York and other North American cities. The crowd includes young toughs and United Nations Ambassadors, dread-locked rastas and churchgoing grandmothers—a virtual cross section of Caribbean America. In recent years, many of the community's more respectable members have complained about the raucousness of the Carnival. Still, they continue to come, and to bring their American-born children.

In Brooklyn and elsewhere, Carnival is a time when people play with the idea of identity: it is a moment when one can question and redefine "who one is." It is fitting that Carnival has become the most visible public symbol of New York's West Indian community at the historical moment when that community is redefining itself. Like the West Indian community, Brooklyn's Carnival is now too massive to ignore, and thus serves to make visible a group of people who, caught between their status as Blacks in a racially divided city and as immigrants distinct from the larger African-American community, have long felt invisible (see Bryce-Laporte 1972). A festival full of uncertainties and contradictions, Carnival also presents an appropriately ambiguous public face for a people whose role in the city's civic life has long been in flux.

It is this state of internal flux that makes Carnival a dynamic and important arena in which various ideas may be put forward in the playful guise of celebration. Like its diaspora cousin, the London Carnival studied by Abner Cohen (1980a, 1982), it is a "contested terrain," a unique social space in which social and political reality are subject to redefinition. Thus, Carnival is a sphere in which the potential for both conformist and oppositional politics is always present simultaneously. It is not merely a reflection of politics—in a very real sense it *is* politics, a realm where new ideas about power relations may be articulated in the context of a public drama.

Carnival Comes to Brooklyn

Carnival in Trinidad served as a model for the Brooklyn celebration, as well as those in Toronto and London. The former emerged in the eighteenth century as the pre-Lenten fete of Trinidad's largely Catholic plantocracy, but the ex-slaves took it over following emancipation. From the late nineteenth century on, Carnival was marked by masquerades, the ritualized violence of *calinda* stick fighting, and satiric calypso music. On several occasions it was also a time of violent confrontations between the poor and the authorities (Pearse 1956). By the mid-twentieth century, highly competitive neighborhood steelbands, a cross between dance orchestras and street gangs, became the central organizing force of the Carnival (Brown 1990; Aho 1987). At the same time the island's business leaders sought to use the focus on music to gain control of the event and transform it into something more compatible with the emerging tourist industry (Powrie 1956).[2] After independence in 1962, Carnival also became a source of nation-building for a status-conscious elite who paradoxically took its cultural cues from the poor and converted the latter's symbols of equality into expressions of national unity in an otherwise profoundly stratified society (Hill

1972). Trinidad is traditionally a source of employment for persons from smaller islands. Thus, over the years, Trinidad's Carnival forms and traditions were spread by returning migrants to parts of the Caribbean that had their own Carnival traditions, as well as to Protestant territories in which the pre-Lenten fete was unknown. Since World War Two Trinidadian migrants have carried their Carnival to New York, Toronto, and London, where the event has become a crucial symbol of group identity (Manning 1984; Cohen 1980a, 1982).

New Yorkers from Trinidad and neighboring islands have held small, privately sponsored pre-Lenten dances since the 1920s, as well as modest, outdoor street Carnivals in Harlem as early as the mid-1930s (Hill 1994). In 1947 Jesse Wardle, a Trinidadian immigrant, obtained a parade permit for a Carnival procession from 110th Street to 142nd Street in Harlem. Held on Labor Day, a time of year more suitable than February for outdoor celebrations in New York, this event was sponsored by Congressman Adam Clayton Powell (interestingly, one of the few prominent New York black politicians of the period who was *not* of Caribbean descent). News of the Harlem event soon traveled back to the islands via the "poor man's newspaper" of calypso:

> Labor Day I felt happy,
> because I played Carnival in New York City.
> Seventh Avenue was jumpin',
> everybody was shakin'.
> From 110th to 142nd,
> We had bands of every description...
> This is the first time New York ever had,
> Carnival on the streets like Trinidad.[3]

Although based on the Trinidad model and dominated by Trinidadian organizers, this street Carnival was from its inception self-consciously pan-West Indian. Caribbean unity, albeit on Trinidadian terms, was a central theme. The sheer numbers of people involved in such a highly visible event helped to promote a sense of group identity. Scheduling the event on Labor Day helped to break the always tenuous connection to Catholicism of the pre-Lenten Carnival and facilitated the participation of West Indians of all religions.

In 1964, following a bottle-throwing incident between African Americans and Caribbean revelers (coming on the heels of a more serious outbreak of violence in 1961), the parade permit for Carnival in Harlem was revoked. Rufus Gorin, a Trinidad-born masquerade bandleader and longtime participant in the Harlem Carnival, attempted to organize a new Labor Day Carnival in Brooklyn, where large numbers of West Indian immigrants had settled. The small *ad hoc* committee he headed initially met resistance from the city, which was hesitant to sponsor a large street gathering of Blacks during that riot-torn period. Then, in 1971, a group headed by Carlos Lezama, a Trinidadian immigrant and machinist for the New York City Transit Authority, obtained permission to hold Carnival on Eastern Parkway, Frederick Law Olmstead's massive boulevard that runs through the heart of central Brooklyn's black neighborhoods.[4] The broad Parkway is uniquely suited to the huge event, although one can hardly imagine a use more distant from Olmstead's stately vision.

The number of West Indians in New York had already begun to swell following the 1965 immigration reforms. Over the next three decades, the community and the event grew together. The area immediately south of Eastern Parkway—which some in the community are now campaigning to have renamed "Caribbean Parkway"— soon became the cultural and demographic center of West Indian settlement in New York. The committee, still headed by Lezama, is now a permanent organization known as the West Indian American Day Carnival Association (WIADCA).

Despite its massive growth, the format of Brooklyn's Carnival has changed little over the years. During the week prior to Labor Day Monday a series of concerts, steelband contests, and children's pageants are held on the grounds of the Brooklyn Museum. The events climax with a huge Carnival procession on Eastern Parkway on Labor Day itself. These "official" Carnival activities are accompanied by dozens of affiliated dances, concerts, and parties in West Indian neighborhoods around the city.

In sharp contrast to most of New York's numerous "ethnic" festivals, the Carnival lacks a centralized structure. The WIADCA obtains the needed permits and deals with city officials, yet its members are more coordinators than leaders. The dozens of dances, shows, and parties throughout the city that complement the parade are run by individual promoters who operate independently of the WIADCA. The various steelbands and "mas" (masquerade) bands are all privately organized, and their leaders are frequently at odds with the Association.

Each mas band is composed of several dozen to several hundred elaborately costumed revelers who dance to live or recorded music in the Carnival procession. They are loosely organized around themes that emphasize fantasy ("Galactic Splendor," "Splendors of

the Far East," "Party in Space"), ethnicity ("Caribbean Unite"), or
current events ("Cry for Freedom," "Tribute to Bob Marley"). Historical themes, with costumes influenced by Hollywood epics ("Ex-
tracts from Rome") are particularly popular, as are those which use
popular culture references in bizarre juxtapositions. In 1990, for
example, one band used the theme "Ponderosa in Hell." Its masqueraders, clad in black and red, wore cowboy hats, toy six-guns,
tin stars, devil masks and wings. In general, costumes are loosely
coordinated but by no means uniform. In some bands all members
are in costume, although in most only a few members wear elaborate outfits while the majority simply wear matching tee shirts. All
bands, however, feature at least one or two (and often a dozen) ex-
tremely complex and fantastic outfits that are not so much costumes as small, one-person floats.

Carnival costumes on Eastern Parkway, Brooklyn. Photo by Ernest Brown.

The leaders of these bands invest a tremendous amount of time
and energy in Carnival preparations. Sponsoring a band is expen-
sive, and while most of the leaders can be described as "middle
class," none is wealthy. Yet, they frequently report investing thousands of dollars out of pocket for band expenses. Although some of
this money is recouped through the sale of costumes, at best the
bands break even, and many lose money. While the leaders may be
involved in preparations throughout the year, the costume makers

usually start to work in the early summer, with work coming to a feverish pitch in the month preceding the Carnival. Typically this work—men constructing the mechanical parts of costumes, women sewing—takes place in rented storefronts, basements, social clubs and private homes. Costume design has occasionally been subsidized by grants from the National Endowment for the Arts and the New York State Council on the Arts. Community leaders not only feel such funding is appropriate, but often express the view that it is insufficient compared with other cultural events in the city, or with the large state-sponsored budget for Carnival in Trinidad.

In the actual Labor Day procession each masquerade band half marches and half dances around a flatbed truck that may carry a calypso group or a steelband, but in recent years has been more likely to sport a huge sound system playing recorded calypso or soca music. The trucks display banners announcing the name of the band's leader, its theme and its sponsors (usually local businesses or politicians), and occasionally social service organizations or labor unions. Sometimes the vehicle itself becomes part of the display: a local shipping company decorates its delivery van as an outrageous version of a cargo ship, complete with shipping barrels on the roof. The bands remain completely independent of and in competition with each other.

The lack of central organizational authority is evident in the form of the Carnival parade itself. The procession starts around noon with a group of dignitaries, grand marshals (usually local business leaders, celebrities and politicians), and city officials who march, or rather saunter, down the Parkway. But they do not draw much attention, for the main body of the Carnival may be a mile or even two miles behind them. Next come several carloads of West Indian-American beauty contest winners who are likewise largely ignored. The crowds that line the Parkway eating, drinking and talking to friends, show little interest in these "parade" elements that are grafted rather uneasily onto the Carnival form.[5]

The real Carnival begins when more than a dozen large masquerade bands, surrounding flatbed trucks carrying musicians or sound systems, start down Eastern Parkway, theoretically in order. This structure breaks down almost immediately. Bands stop, change direction, or simply get bogged down in a dancing mass of humanity. The distinction between participant and spectator quickly disappears, despite the concerted efforts of the police to maintain it. Some bands do not even finish the three-mile route in the allotted six hours. As a dramatic event, Carnival is strikingly leaderless. There are themes and a certain ebb and flow, but no particular center or head.

Community leaders and politicians seeking local recognition and support are naturally attracted to huge gatherings like Carnival. Yet the event itself subverts notions of leadership and presents a throng of autonomous individuals. This presents politicians and even the WIADCA officials with a dilemma: how does one "lead" an event without a head or even a very clear direction? In recent years both politicians and the WIADCA have tried to tighten Carnival's organization; as the event has grown they have urged a more rigorous schedule to allow the maximum number of bands to make it down the Parkway. This became a critical issue in 1995, when two hours of the event were covered on live television. Further, after the Crown Heights disturbances in 1991, the increased police presence at Carnival succeeded in dampening the more chaotic elements of the event. On the whole, however, efforts to remake Carnival more in the mold of a traditional ethnic parade have met with only modest success.[6]

Carnival and the Construction of Ethnic Identity

Brooklyn's Carnival is clearly an "ethnic" event in a city where ethnicity is politically salient. Yet "ethnic" identity functions on a number of different levels. While Carnival clearly asserts a massive presence in New York, it does not offer the opportunity to make a strategic statement: it is too anarchic to be manipulated or to support a structure. Nevertheless, the WIADCA leadership strives to project an image of ethnic distinctiveness and solidarity, and to use Carnival as a means of gaining cultural recognition for Caribbean people in New York City. As Lezama writes:

> To West Indians, as one of the many ethnic minorities in New York, the need for social collaboration, the introduction of a feeling of community and brotherhood are variables critical to us in maintaining our existence within the wider sphere of other ethnic groups (WIADCA souvenir brochure, 1983).

A former Association officer puts it more directly: "We expect the powers that be to recognize Carnival as part of our culture, as the culture of any other group is recognized."[7]

The notion that West Indians are an ethnic group like other ethnic groups implies the presence of clearly recognized political leaders to whom the "powers that be" can pay deference and who may serve as brokers between the state and the ethnic population.[8] The WIADCA presents itself as such a group, and the "powers that be"— often far more comfortable with the cultural assertions of black immigrants than with the more oppositional stances of many black natives—have obliged. Since the mid-1970s, mayors and governors have favored the WIADCA with proclamations, symbolic tributes, and City Hall receptions. Ironically Carnival itself tends to subvert these efforts. In its satirization of power and hierarchy, Carnival undermines the authority of its own organizers and the political officials from whom it seeks "recognition." Most people in the great throng do not know Lezama's name and few recognize him in the crowd. The other WIADCA leaders are even more anonymous as they attempt to lead an event that stubbornly refuses to be led. It is the stilt walker, the devil man, the mas bandleader, the pan player, and the calypsonian who stand out and who will be remembered.

But if Carnival does not create group leaders, it does assert group boundaries. More than any other event it visibly embodies the emerging pan-West Indian identity now evident in New York. As the calypsonian Mighty Sparrow says:

> You can be from St. Cleo, or from John John,
> in New York, all that done.
> They haven't to know who is who,
> New York equalize you.
> Bajan, Grenadian, Jamaican, "toute monde,"
> drinking they rum, beating they bottle and spoon.
> Nobody could watch me and honestly say,
> they don't like to be in Brooklyn on Labor Day![9]

This assertion of a pan-West Indian identity is one of the reasons why Carnival has become so important in New York, despite the fact that the majority of Afro-Caribbean New Yorkers come from nations with no Carnival tradition. The importance of Carnival lies in the fact that it is unquestionably "ethnic" in form—that is it asserts a distinct cultural heritage. Yet the Carnival tradition of satire, inversion, creativity and innovation leaves the content of this identity unfixed. Carnival creates a space in which a reformulation of identity and a realignment of social relations are possible.

To the extent that Trinidadian symbols have been central to the Carnival, the defining of this new *West Indian* identity takes place on unequal terms. While people from throughout the anglophone Caribbean and Haiti attend Carnival, along with growing numbers of Latinos and African Americans, the WIADCA, the steelbands and the masquerade bands are still dominated by Trinidadians. Carnival is highly developed in Trinidad, and naturally Trinidadians bring with them the skills to mount the festival. Yet this Trinidadian tradition is put forward as an expression of *West Indian* identity. Jamaicans, the largest West Indian population in New York, are particularly underrepresented in Carnival organizations. In part this is because they lack a strong Carnival tradition, and the Jamaican national music, reggae, is in many ways a rival to the Trinidadian calypso that dominates the traditional Carnival.[10] Thus, in New York, Carnival continually vacillates between its Trinidadian roots and its pan-Caribbean agenda. As a Jamaica-born politician who marched in front of the 1984 Carnival put it:

> When you talk about Carnival, three or four different places come to my mind: Trinidad, Panama, Venezuela, maybe New Orleans...it's a worldwide thing. They (Trinidadians) transferred it here in their own image. I wouldn't want to take it away from them as such, you know, as being Trinidadian. And yet, you find that now it's blended. You have other groups in it. Any group you will check, you will find all other West Indians participating in it. It's not a Trinidad Labor Day Carnival, it's a Caribbean Labor Day Carnival.[11]

Music has played a central role in the negotiation of cultural politics that occurs during Carnival. In its early years the concerts presented on the Brooklyn Museum grounds featured overwhelmingly Trinidadian entertainers. The 1974 Carnival program lists a steelband competition, an "Ole Mas" competition, a costume competition and a "calypso tent"—all distinctly Trinidadian cultural forms. By 1976, however, the WIADCA—which, as Hill (1994) notes, was still almost entirely Trinidadian—added a "Night in the Caribbean" on the Saturday before Carnival. This concert featured Jamaican reggae, Haitian dance troupes and even a group from Costa Rica. In 1983, in an attempt to include more Jamaicans and more young people in general, the organizers added "Reggae Night" to the festivities on the Thursday night preceding Labor Day. The reggae concert was both part of the Carnival and distinctly separate from the weekend's other events. "The Jamaicans," Lezama noted to the *Jamaican Weekly Gleaner*, 15 August 1983, "wanted their own night." In 1987, a "Haitian Night" was added as well.

Cultural tension between Jamaica and Trinidad, the two largest nations of the Anglophone Caribbean, has a long history. Trinidad, home of the steel drum and calypso and a center for West Indian art, literature, and dance, was clearly the dominant force during the early postwar era. During this period Jamaican popular music was largely derived from Trinidadian and African-American styles, and Jamaican culture in general was under the influence of the

The BWIA Sonatas Steel Orchestra at the West Indian Labor Day Carnival celebration on Eastern Parkway, Brooklyn, 1977. Photo by Marilynn Yee, courtesy of The New York Times.

United States. The 1960s, however, saw the evolution of two distinctly Jamaican cultural forms—Rastafarianism and reggae music—that provided the language for a new flowering of Jamaican culture. By the decade's end both had burst forth from the slums of West Kingston, exerting influence on Jamaicans of all social classes, as well as young people throughout the region and throughout the world. Thus, while a split between the advocates of calypso and reggae music in the London and New York Carnivals started as a Trinidadian-Jamaican conflict, by the late 1970s it had also come to overlap with a generational split within the community.

Ironically, while the lyrics of reggae music (and the Rastafarian philosophy that helped shape it) are militantly pan-Africanist, its musical form, with its rhythmic use of electric guitars and vocal harmonies, is strongly influenced by American and British rock music. Reggae is thus quite accessible to young North Americans and Europeans. The conspicuous use of marijuana (a sacramental plant for believing Rastas) by many leading reggae musicians also helped win acceptance of the rock audience. While respectable middle-class members of West Indian societies had long looked to

Britain for their notions of cultural propriety, young people from the lowest strata of Caribbean society were gaining wide acclaim in Britain, in part because they flaunted the most disreputable of lower-class Jamaican habits: ganja smoking.

By contrast, calypso and its more recent popular derivative, soca,[12] while seen as more respectable in the Caribbean, are often less accessible to European and North American listeners. The music is faster and more percussive, using blaring brass rather than guitars for rhythmic accents. Both reggae and calypso songs are often about sex, but the latter tend to be more humorous and bawdier. Reggae's politics lean toward the messianic and revolutionary in a very general sense, while calypsonians make pointed political statements, topical commentaries, and satires on specific people and local events.

By the early 1990s "classic" reggae had also started to be eclipsed. Less melodic, bass line driven Jamaican "dance hall" music, which has both influenced and been heavily influenced by African-American rap, is now the most popular sound among the young.

These divisions can all be seen on Eastern Parkway on Labor Day. In the late 1970s Hill and Abrahamson (1980) observed that young reggae fans tended to group around sound systems at one end of Eastern Parkway and on side streets, listening to recorded music, while Trinidad-style street "jump up" predominated in the middle of the Carnival throng. Of course not all young reggae fans are Jamaican. However, many young New York West Indians choose to express themselves in the Jamaican mode, just as their elders tend to articulate their ethnicity in terms of Trinidadian origin. By the 1980s a few reggae bands mounted on trucks joined in the procession, and both reggae and soca could be heard throughout the Parkway. In the 1990s soca dominated the mas bands, but it was contemporary reggae and dance hall music that poured out of the windows and the sound systems set up along the side streets.

While the WIADCA has sought to encourage the participation of all West Indians, it continues to define the "real" Carnival traditions in Trinidadian terms. The Association and other Trinidadian groups have sought funding to train young United States-born West Indians in such skills as costume making and steelband music, thus promoting their own particular definition of West Indian culture. They have also sponsored an annual "Kiddie Carnival," held during the afternoons preceding the Saturday and Sunday night Carnival shows. Children compete for prizes for the best costumes and dance to calypso on the big stage as proud parents fawn and flashbulbs click. The WIADCA sees these events as ways to pass on "ethnic traditions" to the young, yet Carnival, with its overtones of sexuality, is difficult to adapt for children. The sanitized children's version conforms, in some ways, to the spirit of North American notions of "ethnic" culture rather than the West Indian Carnival tradition. Still, for many middle-aged parents, Kiddie Carnival is a far more acceptable version of West Indian culture than the Rasta-influenced, Jamaican-based hybrid of the late 1970s or the gangsta-rap-influenced versions of dance hall music favored by the youth of the 1990s.

In the late 1980s, leaders of steelbands who were often at odds with the Association and the mas bands, took their own step toward restoring the "authentic" Trinidadian roots of Carnival. Tired of being literally drowned out by the recorded music from the sound trucks that now dominate Eastern Parkway on Labor Day, they created their own central Brooklyn procession.[13] Known as J'Ouvert ("break of day"), the parade starts at 3:00 A.M. on Labor Day morning, a time when nothing is likely to drown out the steelbands. Even at that hour the J'Ouvert celebration draws thousands of revelers, many of whom will later make their way to the more pan-Caribbean Eastern Parkway event.[14]

Carnival and Politics

The underlying ambiguity of the West Indian community's relationship with the rest of black New York comes to the surface in the Carnival. Despite frequent talk of black unity and allusions to Pan-Africanism, Carnival, by its nature, differentiates West Indians from other Blacks. The early organizers believed that these differences should remain within a narrowly defined "cultural" realm. Carnival provided an arena where they might be expressed far more directly than they could be in the realm of government and politics. In recent years, however, politics has come more openly into the Carnival. In 1984, New York's leading black radio station, WLIB, arranged a Carnival appearance by the Reverend Jesse Jackson. The following year a number of politicians (only a few West Indian) seized upon Carnival as an opportunity to get their message across and had undertaken partial sponsorship of mas bands so that their names would appear on the band trucks. Thus, signs saluting "City Councilwoman Rhoda Jacobs" and the "Greater Flatbush Independent Democratic Club" and urging "Andrew Stein for City Council President," "Roy Innis for Congress" (in 1986), and even "Free South Africa" hung alongside those naming Caribbean bakeries, shipping companies and restaurants. Yet the question of whether Carnival should be explicitly political soon became a source of controversy in the community. As Colin Moore, an activist associated with the left wing of New York's Caribbean leadership, wrote in the *Carib News* in 1985:

...the organizers of the Carnival have not outgrown their parochial roots. The gentlemen from Laventille, Sangre Grande
and Arima still view Carnival as an opportunity to "play mas."
They could not perceive its broader cultural implications or
political significance. As a result of this shortsightedness, this
gerontocracy of aging "mas men" has been unable to impose
the discipline, organization and creativity necessary to transform the Carnival from a Laventille affair into a Caribbean
event, from a Brooklyn road march into a citywide media
event, from a backyard bacchanal into a significant political
event.

A few years later, tragic events would, indeed, turn Carnival into a
political event, whether the "aging mas men" wanted it so or not.

Since its early days the Brooklyn Carnival had survived several
attempts by Hasidic Jews of the Lubavitcher sect, whose World
Headquarters is on the Eastern Parkway along the Carnival route,
to have it banned or moved. Despite widespread feeling in the Caribbean community that the small Hasidic community wielded power
far out of proportion to its numbers in Crown Heights, the Jewish
group had been notably unsuccessful in these efforts. Ironically the
Hasidim's resistance to the festival may have actually helped the
West Indian community make inroads with local politicians. For
example, when plans for the event were challenged in 1983 and
1984, the local State Senator, Marty Markowitz, intervened on behalf of the WIADCA. Markowitz, a Jewish representative of a largely
black Caribbean district, then became a grand marshal of the 1984
and 1986 Carnivals and has continued to attend annually. Throughout the 1980s the numbers of both Caribbean and Hasidic residents
grew in Crown Heights, and tensions over real estate, crime, and
the actions of Hasidic security patrols often strained relations between the groups. Yet by and large they lived together peacefully, if
not amicably.

Then on August 19, 1991, a car driven by an Hasidic Jew—part
of the Lubavitch Rebbe Menachem Schneerson's motorcade—
jumped a curb in Crown Heights, killing a seven-year-old Guyanese
boy named Gavin Cato and critically injuring his cousin. Rumors,
never substantiated, quickly spread throughout the neighborhood
that a Hasidic ambulance service had ignored the children while
rushing the uninjured driver from the scene. Several hours later a
group of about twenty black youths fatally stabbed a Hasidic student named Yankel Rosenbaum. Three nights of rioting followed in
which groups of Blacks and Hasidim clashed in the streets, Jewish
families were attacked in their homes, and stores belonging to black,

white, and Asian merchants were looted. Black youths marched to the World Headquarters of the Lubavitcher Hasidic sect on Eastern Parkway, where some hurled rocks and bottles and shouted anti-Semitic slogans. Mayor Dinkins, who repeatedly called for calm, was briefly trapped by rock-throwing black youths during a condolence call on the Cato family.

By week's end a massive police presence had quelled the violence, yet the anger remained on both sides. At a loss to explain the outburst in the generally stable Caribbean community, some observers attributed the violence to young people "from the projects" spurred on by "outside agitators"—in other words, to an African-American "underclass." This analysis was half true at best. While most of the Caribbean community was horrified by the violence, many youth in the streets were immigrants and their grievances went far beyond the accident. "This is like trench town," a Jamaican teenager told reporter David Kocieniewski of *New York Newsday*, 24 August 1991. "The wicked and the rich have had their day. Now we can stand up and be heard." In fact, one of the most shocking things about Crown Heights was that many of the rioters could not be dismissed as part of any pathological "underclass"; resentment of the Hasidim seemed just as common among home-owning, middle-class Caribbean immigrants as among poor Blacks, whether native or foreign-born.

Many of the Caribbean community's leaders, while denouncing the violence and condemning anti-Semitism, gave voice to their own longstanding grievances against the Hasidim. The easy equivalence they drew between the accident and the murder revealed the depth of their sense of historical injustice. For their part, the Hasidic leadership saw the killing as only the latest chapter in their own narrative of victimization. They were quick to describe the Crown Heights events as a "pogrom" and even to draw comparisons to Kristallnacht. Both "sides"—if one can talk about "sides" in a riot—perceived themselves as victims. Thus, despite the tragic events that triggered the riot, empathy was in critically short supply.

The African-American activists who dominated media coverage of the Crown Heights events proved more effective as lightning rods for popular discontent than the Caribbean leadership. But, as tempers cooled, many in the Caribbean community came to see these activists as exploiting a tragic situation. In addition, one of the most visible, Sonny Carson, hurt his own cause with clumsy attempts at ethnic politics, such as unfurling a Guyanese flag at Gavin Cato's funeral.

The Crown Heights riot occurred less than two weeks before Labor Day. Understandably, city officials viewed the prospect of hundreds of thousands of Carnival revelers on Eastern Parkway with considerable trepidation. Hasidic leaders called once more for the event to be canceled, and some politicians friendly with the organizers quietly suggested that it might be moved to a less charged location. Yet the organizing committee insisted that Carnival should go forward on Eastern Parkway, as always. "Nothing is going to happen!" Lezama insisted on the Thursday before Labor Day. "I am going to walk down the Parkway and if the head Rabbi wants to come with me, he is welcome! This is what the city needs now!" (Lezama 1991)

Going ahead with Carnival was an enormous risk. Violence would gravely threaten its future and any overture to the Hasidim would certainly be attacked by some in the black community as a sell out ("a shame before God" is how Sonny Carson described it). Yet Lezama, who has made the Carnival his life's work, understood the community. He put aside years of bad feelings and invited representatives of the Hasidic community to join the event. To the surprise of many, they accepted. On Labor Day the crowd was a bit more subdued than usual, but it greeted the Rabbis politely, and the day came off without incident: "Peace on the Parkway" was the year's slogan. The deep wounds that drive New York's racial politics were not healed, or even forgotten. Yet, for most of the people on the Parkway, two weeks of tension had been enough. For one day, at least, peace on the Parkway seemed like a good idea.

The ambivalence with which the Caribbean community viewed the riot was, not surprisingly, best captured in a calypso. In 1992 the Mighty Sparrow's "Crown Heights Justice" was among the most memorable songs of that year's Trinidad Carnival, and the following Labor Day it could be heard throughout central Brooklyn. On the one hand it was a call for peace:

> Why do we have this confrontation?
> Violence will not solve our situation.
> We must learn to live in peace,
> live in Peace!
> Preacherman, Rabbi, Priest,
> live in Peace!

And he invoked harmony between Blacks (particularly West Indians) and Jews:

> History will show from slavery to holocaust,
> the whole world know, so we have to live in peace...

No reason to fight like beasts; live in peace!
Pain and suffering we have borne,
Blacks and Jews should live as one,
and celebrate; here life is great!
No Swastika.
No slave master.
Instead we fight the endless fight,
where we live here in Crown Heights...

Yet reiteration of long standing grievances follows this call for harmony:

My reason for being upset is plain to see,
the special treatment you get from Albany...
No cops on my block to complain to—
But police around the clock to protect you—from who?

The song's refrain put the emphasis on justice, along with a quote from Marcus Garvey:

All we want is Justice!
Don't deny the Justice!
All the excuses, all the lies,
can't stifle the children's cries.
For the little boy who died,
and the little girl who cried,
Ethiopia will rise—again!...
The system is pregnant with fault,
but it mustn't fail.
Guilty drivers go to jail!
That's what we call justice![15]

Conspicuous by its absence was any mention of "justice" for the Hasidic scholar who died not by accident but at the hands of an angry mob.

In 1994 controversy with the Hasidic community arose again, with the convergence of Labor Day and Rosh Hashanah. Again Lezama rebuffed attempts by city officials to have the event rescheduled. He and other West Indian community leaders argued that Carnival might not be as old as Rosh Hashanah, but it was no less important and should be treated with the same respect. Yet once the City assured the continuation of the event on the Parkway, Lezama went out of his way to reassure the Hasidic leadership that the event would end on time, and to coordinate the activities of the two communities in a less confrontational manner. Some members of the Hasidic community could not be placated, while some Caribbeans and African-Americans criticized Lezama for being overly solicitous of Hasidic support. Yet the majorities in both communities seemed satisfied, if not completely happy, with the division of scarce public spaces at these sacred times of the year.

The controversy, however, resulted in increased media attention. Carnival has given the New York media the opportunity to review the state of the Caribbean community and to question the identity of a people who are both black and immigrant in a city usually divided between Blacks and immigrants. And the peaceful end of the 1994 controversy appealed to the media's comfort with ethnic celebration over racial confrontation. Thus in 1995, two hours of Carnival were televised live for the first time, and the Lezama's "aging mas men" occupied center stage. Carnival's particular version of pan-Caribbean ethnic identity enjoyed a uniquely prominent position in the community's efforts to define itself.

Will younger, more assertive leaders handle such issues differently? As second-generation Caribbean New Yorkers take over Carnival, will they make it into something more in keeping with the typical "ethnic parade," along the lines of St. Patrick's Day or the Puerto Rican Day parades? It is, of course, too early to say. For now, Carnival remains the place for presenting and dramatizing the idea of a Caribbean community in New York. So long as its form remains in flux, it will continue to provide the social and temporal space in which notions of group identity can be played with, contested, and worked out. It will continue to interest sociologists (or at least *this* sociologist) who are trying make sense of the changing ethnic landscape in an increasingly global city.

NOTES

1. Portions of this essay have been previously published in Philip Kasinitz, *Caribbean New York: Black Immigrants and the Politics of Race* (Ithaca: Cornell University Press, 1992).

2. This period in the development of the Trinidad Carnival is marvelously captured in Earl Lovelace's 1979 novel, *The Dragon Can't Dance.*

3. "Labor Day," Folkways Records 06914, recorded by Lord Invader, 1955.

4. Lezama was actually born in Venezuela, to Trinidadian parents. Like many English-speaking West Indian immigrants born in Spanish speaking nations, he considers himself West Indian, not Latino.

5. Manning (1984) notes a similar situation at the Bermuda National Cricket Championships where the "action" on the sidelines, gambling and the display of the latest fashions, often "upstages" the cricket games themselves.

6. For more on the contrast between Carnival and New York's ethnic parades, see Freidenberg and Kasinitz (1990).

7. Confidential source, personal interview by author (1987).

8. For a fascinating theoretical account of this notion of "recognition"—as opposed to the redistribution of resources—as the basis of claim for justice, see Fraser (1995).

9. "Mas in Brooklyn," Recording Artists Productions, composed and recorded by the Mighty Sparrow, 1976.

10. In Toronto reggae has become an important feature of the Carnival and reggae events are often among the best attended, a fact the Jamaican press reports with some pride, although this is in part due to large numbers of young whites who attend these events. In London, the calypso/reggae split has divided Carnival along generational lines. Cohen (1980a) reports that since 1976 reggae recorded music has come to dominate the event, although young West Indians seem to be mixing both Trinidad masquerades and Jamaican music into a new synthesis. Cohen's (1982) work on the earlier period of the London Carnival illustrates how beneath the presentation of unity public festivals may be contested terrain between groups and sub-groups.

11. Confidential source, personal interview by author (1987).

12. Soca is a shortened form of "Soul-Calypso" and is a fusion of traditional calypso and African-American popular dance music.

13. In Trinidad, the home of the steel pan, steel orchestras have for decades been losing out to sound trucks with recorded music. However, the steel orchestras still maintain a strong Carnival presence at the J'Ouvert celebration and the state-sponsored panorama competition. See Stuempfle (1995, 194-206).

14. For more on the recently instituted J'Ouvert celebration in Brooklyn see Allen and Slater's essay in this volume.

15. "Crown Heights Justice," Charlies Records 004, composed and recorded by the Mighty Sparrow, 1992.

REFERENCES CITED

Aho, William R. 1987. "Steelband Music in Trinidad and Tobago: The Creation of a People's Music." *Latin American Music Review* 8 (1): 26-58.

Bakhtin, Mikhail. 1968. *Rabelais and His World*. Cambridge, MA: MIT Press.

Brown, Ernest. 1990. "Against the Odds: The Impact of Social Forces on Carnival, Calypso and Steelband in Trinidad." *Black Perspectives in Music* 18: 81-100.

Bryce-Laporte, R.S. 1972. "Black Immigrants: The Experience of Invisibility and Inequality." *Journal of Black Studies* 3: 29-56.

Cohen, Abner. 1980(a). "Drama and Politics in the Development of a London Carnival." *Man* 15: 65-86.

_____1980(b). *The Politics of Elite Culture: Explorations in the Dramaturgy of Power*. Berkeley: University of California Press.

_____1982. "A Polyethnic London Carnival as a Contested Cultural Performance." *Ethnic and Racial Studies* 5: 22-41.

Da Matta, Roberto. 1979. *Carnavais, Malandros E Herois*. Rio de Janeiro: Zahar.

Elder, J.D. 1964. "Color, Music and Conflict: A Study of Aggression in Trinidad with Reference to the Role of Traditional Music." *Ethnomusicology* 8: 129-136.

Fraser, Nancy. 1995. "Redistribution and Recognition: A Critique of Justice Truncated." *New Left Review*.

Freidenberg, Judith, and Philip Kasinitz. 1990. "Los Rituales Publicos y la Politizacion de la Etnicidad en Nueva York." *Desarrollo Economico*, No. 117 (Junio): 109-132.

Hall, Herman. 1982. "Inside Brooklyn's Carnival." *Everybody's Magazine*, November.

Hill, Donald, and Robert Abrahamson. 1980. "West Indian Carnival in Brooklyn." *Natural History* 88: 72-84.

Hill, Donald. 1994. "A History of West Indian Carnival in New York to 1978." *New York Folklore* 20(1-2): 47-66.

Hill, Errol. 1972. *The Trinidad Carnival*. Austin: University of Texas Press.

Kasinitz, Philip. 1992. *Caribbean New York: Black Immigrants and the Politics of Race*. Ithaca: Cornell University Press.

Kasinitz, Philip, and Judith Freidenberg. 1987. "Caribbean Public Celebrations in New York City: The Puerto Rican Parade and the West Indian Carnival." In *Caribbean Life in New York City: Social and Cultural Dimensions*, ed. Constance Sutton and Elsa Chaney, 327-49. Staten Island, NY: Center for Migration Studies.

Lezama, Carlos. 1991. Personal interview by author.

Manning, Frank. 1984. "Symbolic Expression of Politics: Cricket and Carnival." Presented at the Conference in New Perspectives on Caribbean Studies. Hunter College, New York, 30 August.

Moore, Colin. 1985. "Some Reflections on the Labor Day Carnival." *New York Carib News*, 24 September: 15.

Pearse, Andrew. 1956. "Carnival in Nineteenth Century Trinidad." *Caribbean Quarterly* 4: 250-262.

Powrie, B.E. 1956. "The Changing Attitudes of the Colored Middle Class Towards Carnival." *Caribbean Quarterly* 4: 224-32.

Roehler, Gordon. 1984. "Calypso and Social Confrontation in Trinidad: 1970 to Present." Paper presented at the Conference on New Perspectives on Caribbean Studies, Hunter College, 30 August.

Stuempfle, Stephen. 1995. *The Steelband Movement: The Forging of a National Art in Trinidad and Tobago*. Philadelphia: University of Pennsylvania Press.

Turner, Victor. 1983. "The Spirit of Celebration." In *The Celebration of Society: Perspectives on Contemporary Cultural Performance*, ed. Frank Manning, 103-124. Bowling Green, Ohio: Bowling Green University Popular Press.

West Indian American Carnival Day Association, Brooklyn, NY.
    1974. Carnival Program Book.
    1976. Carnival Program Book.
    1977. Carnival Program Book.
    1983. Carnival Program Book.

Steel Pan Grows in Brooklyn
Trinidadian Music and Cultural Identity

Ray Allen and Les Slater

On Labor Day, 1966, a year after new immigration laws opened the gates for Caribbean migration to New York, a young Trinidadian named Winston Monroe arrived at Kennedy Airport. Like many ambitious West Indian immigrants, Monroe had come to the United States with dreams of pursuing his education and establishing a professional career. But Monroe was also a talented steel pan player, and he had heard rumors about the big West Indian-American Carnival celebration that had recently moved from Harlem to Brooklyn. His curiosity was quickly satisfied, as he recalls:

> When I arrived at the airport I was met by a cousin of mine, and he took me directly to the Labor Day parade in Brooklyn, which was on St. John's place at the time. One of the guys had a tenor pan, and I started playing on it, in the parade. We played Sparrow's "Patsy." It wasn't a band, just a group of guys on the truck with one tenor pan, a couple of irons, and a conga drum (Monroe 1996).

A month after this dramatic introduction to Brooklyn Carnival, Winston Monroe was recruited into a small steel-pan ensemble led by Hal Gordon. After playing several engagements for African-American audiences in Newark clubs, the band settled into a regular pattern of performing for predominantly white, middle-class audiences who desired "exotic" island music for their parties and dances. In 1971, after completing a degree at Hunter College and taking an accounting position in a leather importing business, Monroe joined the Pan Masters, a large ensemble that made its debut at the West

Indian-American Carnival celebration that had just moved to Brooklyn's grand boulevard, Eastern Parkway. Unlike his first group, Pan Masters played lively calypso music primarily for dances, fetes (parties), and block parties in Brooklyn's burgeoning West Indian community. By 1974 internal tensions caused the band to split into two units, with Monroe joining the new group called the Silhouettes. The following year the Silhouettes placed second at the newly instituted Labor Day Panorama contest. Bands were springing up everywhere, Monroe recalls, and pan activity seemed to be at an all-time high in Brooklyn.

But by the late 1970s record-spinning deejays and heavily amplified soca (soul-calypso) music were beginning to displace conventional steelbands at West Indian parties, while trucks with ear-splitting sound systems were drowning out even the largest steel orchestras on Eastern Parkway. As the West Indian party circuit dried up, the Silhouettes turned to white audiences for regular weekend engagements. Throughout the late 1970s and 1980s, the Silhouettes, like many Brooklyn-based steelbands, maintained a small "stage-side" unit of ten players for private (mostly white) parties, and expanded to fifty or more players for the West Indian Carnival Panorama, which took place at a special pre-Labor Day evening concert behind the Brooklyn Museum.

In 1996, thirty years after his arrival in Brooklyn, Monroe continues to manage and occasionally play with the Silhouettes. Although disturbed that pan has been replaced in many arenas by electric ensembles and pre-recorded music, he is optimistic that New York steel pan music is making a resurgence in the 1990s. He speaks proudly of the steelband instructional program he oversees at Brooklyn's Intermediate School 232. And the Brooklyn *J'Ouvert* (early morning) Carnival celebration, instituted recently to showcase steelbands, provides a fresh new performance venue that he believes will help reinvigorate the tradition.

Winston Monroe was not the first Trinidadian to "beat pan" in Brooklyn, nor the most influential. But his career as a panman illustrates the triumphs and frustrations experienced by members of New York's steel pan movement. Over the years many culturally minded Trinidadian New Yorkers have embraced steel pan music with pride, particularly during Carnival season. Yet lack of community financial support, and the desire for broader recognition and monetary gain, led many pan players to focus their attention on a wider, whiter audience. Examining the role of steel pan in New York's Trinidadian community, as well as the instrument's ability to cross cultural boundaries, reveals much about the relationship between musical expression and social identity for urban immigrants.[1] Before turning to these broader issues, the origins of the steel pan and its place in Trinidadian society will be considered.

Steel Pan in Trinidad

Contrary to popular myth, steel pan music did not spring spontaneously from the streets of Port of Spain when the United States Navy discarded empty fifty-five gallon oil drums in Trinidad following the close of World War Two. The roots of this music stretch back to nineteenth-century percussion traditions associated with Carnival in Trinidad. When the British authorities outlawed skin drumming during Carnival festivities in the mid-1880s, Afro-Trinidadians responded by creating new percussion instruments from different sized pieces of bamboo. By the turn of the century these *tamboo bamboo* bands were providing lively percussion accompaniments for groups of costumed revelers who danced and sang in Port of Spain's grand pre-Lenten Carnival celebration (Stuempfle 1995, 19-31).

Sometime in the mid-1930s tamboo bamboo bands began experimenting with paint and trash cans, biscuit drums, automobile brake drums, and other metal objects. By 1940 metallic percussion instruments were replacing bamboo in the Carnival bands. It was during this period that players discovered that different notes could be produced by pounding the bottoms of metal containers into different shapes and striking them with sticks. By the end of World War Two, these new "steel" bands were providing a polyrhythmic accompaniment for bands of Carnival singers and beating out simple three- and four-note melodies of popular calypso tunes. The transformation of metal containers from percussion devices to melody-producing instruments was underway (Stuempfle 1995, 32-44).

In the early post-war years steel pan tuners (builders) began to forge instruments from oil drums cut into different sizes to produce different tonal ranges. More sophisticated techniques were developed for grooving the notes, leading to pans capable of producing fully chromatic scales and conventional Western harmonies. Thanks to these innovations, steel pan orchestras could, by the 1950s, play more complex arrangements of calypsos as well as Latin dance music, American popular songs, and European classical pieces (Stuempfle 1995, 108-109). Steel orchestras grew in size, and today include as many as 100 performers playing a range of pans divided into six or seven sections. The high-range tenor pans usually play the primary melodic line while the double tenors and double seconds double the melody or contribute counter melodies. The mid-range cello and guitar pans provide chordal accompaniment. Full-sized, fifty-five gallon drums, arranged in six, nine, or twelve drum per player configurations, maintain a moving bass line. A trap drummer, one or more conga drummers, an iron (automobile brake drum struck with a metallic stick) player, and other hand percussionists add a dense, polyrhythmic accompaniment.

Steel pan became a vital art form in colonial Trinidad, and continued to grow after the island gained independence from Great Britain in 1962. Originally scorned as crude street culture associated with prostitution and violence (Slater 1996), pan music was eventually embraced by the middle class. The new post-colonial government consciously promoted steel pan as a symbol of Trinidadian national pride, and bands began receiving government and business support (Stuempfle 1995, 141-150). In 1963 the government established a formal "Panorama" competition as part of the Carnival celebration. By the mid-1960s, just as changes in United States immigration laws were generating a wave of West Indian emigration, Trinidadian steel pan was in its heyday, dominating Carnival processions, fetes, and competitions.

New York Pan Pioneers

The initial diaspora of steel pan music to New York was accomplished through the efforts of a handful of influential Trinidadians who immigrated in the post-war years. Rudy King was the first important pan player to reach New York. When King arrived in Brooklyn in 1949 he was a veteran of Trinidad's Paradise Boys Steel Orchestra, and a skilled pan tuner familiar with the latest techniques of pan construction. He was soon building pans from oil drums in an alley next to his aunt's apartment in Brooklyn's New Lots neighborhood. Within a year he had formed a small group, dubbed appropriately "The Trinidad Steelband," and began playing at West Indian parties, dances, and boat rides. King and five other Trinidad-born musicians each played a single "pan around the neck," and featured a repertory of West Indian calypsos and Latin numbers. After joining the Musicians Union in 1951, King found his band in demand at Greenwich Village clubs and parties for white suburban audiences. He expanded the size of the band, and in the mid-1950s his Trinidadian Steelband became the first steel orchestra to participate in the West Indian Labor Day Carnival held on Lenox Avenue in Harlem. In 1958 King's band was featured in a Carnegie Hall "Steelband Clash" organized by Art D'Lugoff, owner of the Village Gate. King eventually formed the Tropicans, a large orchestra that became a mainstay of the Brooklyn Eastern Parkway Carnival celebration and Panorama contests in the 1970s (King 1996).

Through his tireless efforts as a player, tuner, and bandleader, King helped establish steel pan as a respectable art form in New York's West Indian community, and he introduced the instrument to white American audiences.

Realizing that pan tuning and playing techniques were evolving rapidly in Trinidad during the early 1950s, King sought new arrivals who were familiar with the latest pan developments back home. One such panman was Reynolds "Caldera" Caraballo, a talented player and composer who had grown up in King's neighborhood in Port of Spain. The day Caraballo arrived in 1956 he was recruited into King's band. He eventually formed a small four-piece band for club dates, and in 1958 left King's band to organize another large Brooklyn steel orchestra, Caldera and the Moderneers. His talents as a pan virtuoso did not go unnoticed outside the Trinidadian community, and in the early 1960s he formed another small group, also called the Trinidad Steelband, and toured with the popular Jamaican-American singer Harry Belafonte (Caraballo 1996).

Another native Trinidadian, Conrad Mauge, was introduced to steel pan at jam sessions held in Harlem's Morningside Park in the mid-1950s. He met King at one of these sessions, and soon joined his band in Brooklyn. In 1958 Mauge split from King to form his own band, the Trinidad Serenaders. Unlike King's large orchestra that played primarily for West Indian audiences, Mauge's outfit boasted a wide repertory of popular melodies and catered to white audiences, playing frequently at Greenwich Village clubs (Mauge 1996).

While the King and Caraballo orchestras dominated the Brooklyn scene, in Harlem a New York-born Trinidadian, Lawrence "Pops" McCarthy, was the key figure. In the early 1950s he formed the Harlem All Stars and began playing at Harlem clubs and parties. His band eventually became a regular participant at the annual Lenox Avenue Carnival celebration (Mauge 1996). Following his death in 1977, the *New York Amsterdam News*, 27 August 1977, described McCarthy as a "pioneer of the steelband movement in the United States," noting that under his direction the Harlem All Stars had performed at the Village Gate and toured with Harry Belafonte.

Kim Loy Wong, a Trinidadian of Chinese-African parentage and leader of the Highlanders Steel Orchestra in Port of Spain, immigrated to New York in 1958. He settled in the Lower East Side of Manhattan and soon made his pan playing and building skills available to the University Settlement, a neighborhood community organization. This connection eventually led to his formal affiliation with the New York City Board of Education as a steelband music instructor, where he became a pioneer advocate of steel pan as an educational and recreational activity for inner city youth. In addition he organized a steelband, the Highlanders Steel Orchestra (of New York), which remained headquartered in the Lower East Side until the mid-1960s when it moved to Brooklyn (Hill 1994, 60; Wong 1965). Wong's 1959 and 1961 recordings on the Folkways label—both produced by Pete Seeger—introduced the steel pan to a wider audience of American folk music aficionados.[2]

Another important addition to New York City's growing pan fraternity was Ellie Mannette, who arrived from Trinidad in 1967. Mannette came to New York with the help of Murray Narell, the director of a community center in Manhattan who was aware of Mannette's pioneering efforts as a pan tuner in Trinidad. Mannette soon became tuner for a number of New York bands including the Brooklynaires, the Golden Stars, and Heart and Soul. In addition to building instruments and offering pan instruction (including lessons to Murray Narell's son Andy, later to become an internationally acclaimed pan virtuoso), Mannette founded the Queens-based Trinidad Hummingbirds, a steel orchestra that performed primarily for white audiences at formal concerts and colleges. His exceptional skill as a pan tuner placed him in great demand by schools, community organizations, and individual bands (Hill 1994, 59-60; Mannette 1968).

While these early panmen felt, by and large, a strong allegiance to their Trinidadian roots, the demographics of New York City worked against large-scale community demand for their music. During the 1950s New York's West Indian community was relatively small and offered limited playing opportunities for steelbands at fetes, basement parties, and boat rides. Moreover, many of the West Indian New Yorkers were second generation, and had no contact with the relatively new steelband tradition that was developing in Trinidad. During this period, however, increasing numbers of North Americans were discovering Caribbean music through travel to the islands and through popular calypso recordings. King, Caraballo, Mauge, and other early panmen quickly realized that there was a larger New York audience hungry for their island sounds.

Crossing Over

On 30 December 1954, *House of Flowers*, a humorous musical about rival bordellos on a Caribbean island, opened at Broadway's Alvin Theater. Written by Truman Capote with music by Harold Arlen, the play featured the well-known black American singer Pearl Bailey, Trinidadian dancer Geoffrey Holder, and a steelband trio imported directly from Trinidad. The group, consisting of Michael

Alexander, Alphonso Marshall, and Roderick Clavery (later replaced by Caldero Caraballo), performed lively calypso melodies at various interludes during the play. For the first time *House of Flowers* gave steelband music significant exposure outside of the West Indian community and opened the door for new performance opportunities with white New York audiences. Several promoters, including Village Gate owner Art D'Lugoff, viewed steelband music as an island novelty with great crossover and commercial appeal. The Village Gate, which catered to a predominantly white, arty crowd, was one of the first important night spots to feature live steelband music with groups led by King, Mauge, and Caraballo (Caraballo 1996).

Rudy King (middle pan player) with a small, stage-side version of his Trinidad Steel band playing at the Audubon Ball Room in New York City, circa 1960. Photo courtesy of Rudy King.

Showcasing pan on Broadway and in Village clubs led, not surprisingly, to other engagements in white communities, as bands were approached to play at private suburban parties and country clubs. By the late 1950s, the crossover movement was gaining two other important boosts. One was the New York Musicians Union, which, after King and others joined, became a solid referral source for private engagements (King 1995). The other was the increasing popularity of the Jamaica-American singer Harry Belafonte, whose best-selling recordings introduced millions of non-West Indian listeners to stylized versions of calypsos and Caribbean folk songs. Belafonte tapped into the New York pan community on several occasions in order to incorporate authentic steelband music into his recordings and concert appearances. Caldera Caraballo and Lawrence McCarthy were among the local pan players who became part of the Belafonte entourage during the late 1950s and early 1960s (Caraballo 1996).

The popularity of Belafonte's recordings affected the repertories of steelbands seeking white patronage. Belafonte hits, including "Brown-Skinned Girl," "Mary Ann," "Jamaica Farewell," "Yellow Bird" and "Day-O," along with calypso-tinged arrangements of American popular and jazz standards, became mainstays for bands playing at white parties and country clubs. These small, four-to-six player ensembles, appeared in colorful matching outfits, often with straw hats. Conrad Mauge (1996) recalls that his group, the Trinidad Serenaders, sometimes presented a simple floor show consisting of instrumental calypso standards, sing-along calypsos, and a limbo dance.

The desire to reach mainstream American listeners with familiar tunes is evident in one of the few professional records made by a New York-based steel orchestra. Recorded by the BWIA Sunjet Serenaders Steelband and released by Columbia Records in the mid-1960s, the album featured simple arrangements of American popular standards including "Summertime," "A Taste of Honey," "Maria," "Tonight," "More," and "Theme from Exodus."[3]

King (1995), Caraballo (1996), and Mauge (1996) all report that many bands maintained two distinct repertoires, one for West Indian audiences and another for white ones. While the latter relished Belafonte-style calypso standards, the West Indian audiences demanded the latest Carnival hits from Trinidad. When a steelband arrived at a basement fete, boat-ride party, or Caribbean dance in Manhattan's Audubon Ballroom, it had to be ready with the most recent calypsos by the Mighty Sparrow or Lord Kitchener, and perhaps contemporary Latin and North American numbers (arranged with a calypso beat) that were currently popular in the islands. A steelband would risk ridicule for playing a Belafonte calypso or staging a costumed limbo dance at a Trinidadian fete.

The experiences of Les Slater (co-author of this article) typify the duality of New York's pan scene in the 1960s. Slater arrived from Trinidad in 1964, where he had played and arranged for the popular Highlanders Steel Orchestra. Once in New York he opted to join Conrad Mauge's Trinidad Serenaders, a small ensemble that performed primarily for white audiences. But he also was recruited as an arranger for Kim Loy Wong's Highlanders, a larger band that played primarily for West Indian affairs. Rarely was there any overlap in the two groups' repertoires. The Highlanders were strictly interested in Slater's sophisticated arrangements of the latest tunes from Trinidad—the current year's most popular Carnival calypsos as well as calypso treatments of American popular songs ("Cole Porter Medley"), jazz tunes (Duke Ellington's "Satin Doll"), and European classics with a calypso beat (Beethoven's "Romance in F"). By contrast, the Trinidad Serenaders favored simple, Belafonte-style pop-calypsos and conventional, non-calypso arrangements of American popular songs that conformed to white audiences' expectations of steelband music.

Pan players grew tired of tapping out old calypso standards for white party-goers, but basic economics necessitated such activity. Playing at white parties and clubs, while artistically unchallenging, was simply more lucrative than most West Indian engagements. By all accounts the musicians were well paid and respectfully treated, although some harbored underlying resentment at having to conform to American stereotypes of the colorfully costumed, exotic island drummer (Mauge 1996). But when West Indian party-goers began gravitating toward amplified deejay music in the 1970s, the white circuit continued to prefer small acoustic pan ensembles playing old calypso numbers. Top panmen like King and Caraballo needed to play for white audiences to support their bands, but they saved their most creative efforts for Trinidadian gatherings, and eventually for the ultimate West Indian fete, the annual Labor Day Carnival celebration.

Steel Pan and New York Carnival

Sometime in the mid-1930s two homesick Trinidadians, Rufus Gorin and Jesse Wattle, began organizing outdoor Carnival parties in Harlem. In 1947, Wattle managed to get an official permit to close Lenox Avenue for a Trinidad-style Carnival parade featuring fancy costumed mas (masquerade) bands. In deference to the New York climate, the celebration was held in early September, on the Monday of Labor Day weekend, rather than during the traditional midwinter, pre-Lenten Carnival season (Hill 1994, 48-9; Kasinitz 1992, 140-141).

The early Harlem parade, was, by Trinidadian Carnival standards, relatively conventional. Throughout the 1950s, the *New York Amsterdam News* described the Harlem Carnival as an orderly procession of politicians, dignitaries, beauty queens, floats and costumed dancers.[4] Police barricades separated parade spectators from marchers, with the former numbering as many as 100,000. Panman Caldera Caraballo (1996) recalls the event was "a restricted parade, not really a Carnival," as only invited guests, masquerade bands, and community organizations were allowed to march. Music was provided by conventional American-style marching bands and by Trinidadian brass (calypso) bands perched on floats and small trucks. Calypso singers like MacBeth the Great fronted the brass bands, projecting their voices with the aid of a microphone and small public address system.

Then one Labor Day in the mid-1950s, Rudy King showed up with a band of twenty panmen wearing tee shirts with "Trinidad Steelband" emblazoned across the front. King (1995) recollects performing a simple hymn melody to a calypso beat, with each panman playing a single steel pan strapped around his neck. The crowd on Lenox Avenue was, according to King, quite delighted, and began spontaneously dancing around the orchestra as the panmen moved up the avenue. The following year King returned with a larger group. By the late 1950s, King's band was joined on Lenox Avenue by Lawrence "Pops" McCarthy's Harlem All Stars and Caldera and the Moderneers. These steel orchestras were not officially affiliated with a masquerade band, nor were they formally invited by the parade organizers. King (1995) recalls just "showing up, in the spirit of Carnival." Caraballo (1996) claims the Carnival officials were concerned that steelbands might disrupt the otherwise orderly event: "You see this was a real parade that was trying to start at point A and end at point B," he recalls, "and the steelbands could slow everything down, with all the people coming out on the street and dancing around us. So they kept us in the rear." But the steelbands were tolerated by the organizers because they wanted to showcase authentic Trinidadian culture, and pan had become, by the late 1950s, a central component of the Carnival celebration back home in Port of Spain.

Worries about disruptive behavior became a reality during the 1961 Harlem parade when a fight broke out between a panman and a parade spectator. According to an eyewitness report in the *New York Amsterdam News*, 9 September 1961, a steelband marcher crashed his pan against the head of an overzealous parade-goer who was attempting to grab his instrument. Band members and spectators began to shove one another as bottles and bricks flew. During the ensuing scuffle ten people were arrested for disorderly conduct. The 9 September 1961 headline of the *New York Amsterdam News* proclaimed "West Indian Day Parade Ends in Riot."

Meanwhile, tensions surrounding the burgeoning civil rights movement were making local authorities increasingly wary of large gatherings of black people. Memories of the 1961 disturbance, coupled with a rock throwing incident at the 1964 Harlem Carnival, led to the revocation of the Lenox Avenue parade permit. Rufus Gorin moved to Brooklyn, where he attempted to reestablish a Labor Day Carnival. Following the 1965 immigration reforms, central Brooklyn was rapidly becoming the center of West Indian culture in New York City. For several years annual Carnival celebrations took the form of huge block parties and spontaneous parades in Brooklyn's Crown Heights and Bedford Stuyvesant neighborhoods. But it was not until 1971 that Carlos Lezama, Gorin's successor and head of the newly formed West Indian American Day Carnival Association (WIADCA), succeeded in obtaining a parade permit for Eastern Parkway.

Throughout the late 1960s, prior to the establishment of the Eastern Parkway route, steelbands played informally at Carnival block parties in Crown Heights. In 1971 approximately six steelbands turned out for the first Eastern Parkway event. Several, like Rudy

Rudy King and his Trinidad Steelband playing "pan around the neck" during the 1958 Lenox Avenue Carnival in New York City. Photo courtesy of Rudy King.

King's Tropicans, were relatively small ensembles (twenty to thirty players) whose members still wore single pans strapped around their necks. But Winston Monroe (1996) recalls that his Panmasters featured seventy-five players, many of whom played multiple pans stacked on racks and wagons that were "pulled" up the parkway by fans and costumed dancers. The bands played lively calypso tunes with heavy percussion accompaniment, and provided music for the various masquerade bands whose members "jumped up" (danced) as they processed up the parkway. As in the Harlem parade, lightly amplified brass bands rode on flatbed trucks. Unlike the well ordered Harlem parade, however, the Eastern Parkway celebration was more in keeping with the chaotic revelry that characterized Carnival in Trinidad. The *New York Amsterdam News,* 7 September 1974, reported an "unstructured" event in which "the spectator is at times celebrant; the celebrant spectator." Based on the Trinidadian model, early Eastern Parkway Carnival was a wild spectacle of fancy masquerade bands and steel orchestras jammed together with hundreds of thousands of dancing spectators (see also Hill 1994, 62-64; Kasinitz 1992, 140-159).

The steelbands received no compensation for their appearances on the parkway, although Monroe (1996) recalls the Panmasters being awarded a small trophy for "best steelband performance" at the 1971 Carnival parade. This was in keeping with a longstanding tradition of competition between steelbands in Trinidad. Indeed, by the early 1970s, the Panorama contest in Port of Spain had become the focal point of pan activity (Stuempfle 1995, 157-162). Not surprisingly, there was a move to organize a formal competition as part of the Brooklyn event. Just prior to the 1973 Labor Day Carnival, Horace Morancie, a West Indian who worked with Mayor Lindsay's Model Cities program, was approached by a loosely organized group of steelbands led by Clyde Henry, a former associate of Carlos Lezama. Together Morancie and Henry organized a steel pan contest at Medgar Evers Jr. College, located off Nostrand Avenue in central Brooklyn. Operating independently from Lezama and WIADCA, Morancie and Henry recruited six bands; each group was required to play a calypso and a non-calypso selection. No prize money was offered, but the winning band, the Panmasters, took home a trophy. Morancie and Henry attempted a second pan contest the following year at Boys and Girls High School in Central Brooklyn, but last minute torrential rains resulted in cancellation of the competition (Morancie 1996; Henry 1996).

The success of Morancie's 1973 Medgar Evers College Panorama did not go unnoticed by Lezama and the WIADCA. The organization responded by setting up its own pan competition as part of the

Carnival festivities that took place behind the Brooklyn Museum on Labor Day weekend. The 1974 *West Indian American Day Carnival Association Program Book* lists a "Panorama" event for Friday evening, 30 August, as did a Carnival preview in the *New York Amsterdam News*, 31 August 1974. Rudy King (1995) recalls that his Tropicans took first prize over a handful of competitors, and the 1975 WIADCA program book mentions that the Tropicana Steel Orchestra won the 1974 Panorama contest. But according to Winston Monroe (1996) and Clyde Henry (1996), most of the local steelbands boycotted the 1974 WIADCA-sponsored event and opted to attend Morancie's ill-fated competition at Boys and Girls High School.

Then, in the summer of 1975, Caldera Caraballo was recruited by WIADCA to organize a more elaborate Panorama at the Brooklyn Museum. This time there was no boycott and the event was evidently a huge success. Caraballo (1996) recalls that twelve pan orchestras received small appearance fees and competed for first, second, and third place prize money. The 1976 WIADCA program book contains pictures of nine bands competing in the 1975 Panorama that was won by the Brooklynaires, with the Silhouettes Steel Orchestra and the Sonatas Steel Orchestra coming in second and third place, respectively. The 1977 WIADCA program book reports the 1976 Panorama was won by the Exzibit Serenaders, followed by the Sonatas and the Masqueraders.

By offering prize money and appearance fees, the WIADCA Panorama attracted bands that were no longer willing to compete for a trophy (Morancie 1996). But money remained a contentious issue and relations between WIADCA and the local steelbands were tense. In 1972 Trinidadian-born panman Clyde Henry formed the Steelband Association of the Americas. Henry hoped that by joining together, the steelbands would have a greater say in planning the Labor Day Carnival festivities and that they could lobby the WIADCA for more financial support. In 1973 the SBAA helped Morancie organize the Medgar Evers College Panorama, and in 1974 the organization succeeded in partially boycotting Lezama's initial WIADCA Panorama. The following year Henry resigned and the organization eventually folded (Henry 1996).

The *New York Amsterdam News*, 27 September 1977, reported that a number of steelbands had boycotted earlier Panoramas due to inconsistencies in contracting and awarding prize money. But in that same year prizes of $4000, $2000, and $1000 were offered for first, second, and third place, and according to the paper the event was a success. Squabbles over prize money aside, the WIADCA Panorama competition was established as the centerpiece of Carnival's evening concerts, and eventually was moved to a prime Saturday evening slot, where it remains today.

Steelbands in Brooklyn may have reached their zenith of popularity in the mid-1970s. Pan music was pervasive at the big Eastern Parkway Carnival parade, and the popular Panorama offered bands a chance to compete for fame and fortune. The growing West Indian population was hungry for pan music at fetes, basement parties, and boat rides, while the white club and suburban party circuit continued to offer employment opportunities. But as the decade wore on, new trends in technology and popular music began to spell trouble for pan players and their followers.

Deejays and Sound Systems

Soca, a new pop sound that fused traditional calypso singing with elements of black American soul and disco music, emerged in Trinidad during the mid-1970s, coinciding with a period of economic prosperity driven by the island's expanding oil industry (Manuel 1995, 193-194). Soca's heavy bass lines and mechanical drum rhythms reflected a new musical sensibility favoring high-volume and electronic gadgetry. Record-spinning deejays, broadcasting over powerful sound systems, produced loud, bass heavy dance music that no conventional steelband could come close to matching. When mounted on flatbed trucks, the new sound systems were easily integrated into Carnival street processions. The results were devastating for acoustic steelbands that could not take advantage of the new technology. Deejays rapidly became the favored form of entertainment at fetes and dances, while masquerade bands turned to truck-mounted sound systems for their Carnival music.

Moreover, a more diverse group of singers led the new soca movement. While calypso had been almost exclusively a Trinidadian expression, the new generation of soca stars included Arrow (from Montserrat), Swallow (from Antigua), and Becket (from St. Vincent). Jamaican reggae—another dance music dependent on deejays and high-volume sound systems—was, by the mid-1970s, competing for listeners in Trinidad, throughout the Caribbean, and across the United States. As Jamaican and other non-Trinidadian artists asserted themselves, steel pan was pushed further to the sidelines, pigeonholed as an antiquated musical oddity that was out of place among the electronic trappings of the new soca and reggae.

The advent of large sound systems occurred during a period when Trinidad's steelbands were increasingly devoting their energies and resources to the annual Panorama competition. In the natural progression of things, steelbands, whether deliberately or unwittingly, found themselves canceled out of the party entertainment equation, even at Carnival, a time of accelerated performance activity. Panorama thus became the primary focus of most bands (Stuempfle 1995, 161-164).

The evolving pattern in Trinidad eventually occurred in New York. By the late 1970s, with recorded soca and reggae music becoming ever more attractive to dancers, live pan music at parties began to decline. Powerful sound systems, mounted on huge flatbed trucks, began displacing conventional steelbands on Eastern Parkway. For their part, New York pan practitioners, at least those who looked to their own ethnic community to provide performance opportunities, came to see the Labor Day Carnival Panorama as the main stage for public display of their talent. Throughout the 1980s dissatisfaction continued unabated among the bands over various aspects of the Panorama competition, particularly the issue of prize money. But pan players were hard-pressed to ignore the event, for Panorama had become, for most, the only game in town.

The full scale transplantation of Trinidad's Panorama ritual to New York posed other problems for the steelbands. First, in spite of well-meaning attempts to organize, the steelbands never formed a strong coalition that could have a serious voice in planning and running Brooklyn's Labor Day Panorama competition, as Pan Trinbago did in Trinidad. But more important was the issue of funding. Outfitting a fifty to seventy-five member steel orchestra with instruments and matching tee shirts, and providing a music arranger and transportation for Panorama competition was an immense cost. In Trinidad, corporate sponsorship of steelbands has been the norm since the 1960s, when businesses began lending their dollars and names to prominent bands like the Coca-Cola Desperadoes, the Pan Am North Stars, the Shell Invaders, and the Chase Manhattan Savoys (Stuempfle 1995, 144-145). But with few exceptions—most notably Brooklyn's BWIA Sonatas—New York's steelbands have been unsuccessful in soliciting ongoing corporate sponsorship.

Undeterred by these practical realities, the bands sought to cobble together necessary funds from local West Indian businesses and prominent community leaders. Throughout the 1980s, and into the 1990s, at least a dozen steelbands have turned out annually for Brooklyn's Panorama. The bands complained bitterly about the funding difficulties that hindered their access to professional pan tuners and arrangers, but there were no viable alternatives. Apparently a genuine love of public performance—especially for a Trinidadian audience—and the lure of competition (and prize money) were enough to keep the movement alive.

Reinvigorating Pan in the 1990s

Pan activity in New York appears to be on the upsurge in the 1990s as a new, more diverse generation of players emerges. Following trends in Trinidad, pan has become an increasingly respectable pastime for working- and middle-class West Indian New Yorkers. Ironically, music that was once associated with violent street activity is now promoted by community leaders and educators as a safe and creative recreational activity for young people. A 1997 brochure produced by the Moods Pan Groove Orchestra promises that its youth steel pan program will help students "develop a sense of pride, discipline, and competitiveness," and that "students will become more aware, more responsible, and more willing to stay in school." Pan's improved image has attracted more women to what was once a male dominated activity, and today girls and young women outnumber boys and men in several Brooklyn steel pan orchestras.

The CASYM Steel Orchestra performing at the 1992 Queens Day Festival. Photo by Martha Cooper.

Brooklyn-based community organizations, including the Caribbean American Sports and Cultural Youth Movement (CASYM), the Sesame Flyers International, and the Caribbean-American Steelband Association, sponsor youth steelbands as part of their larger community outreach programming. Each of these organizations offers steel pan lessons for young people (ages eight through eighteen) and coordinates after-school steel pan programs at several Brook-

lyn middle schools and high schools. As pan becomes institutional-
ized in schools and community centers, it reaches growing numbers of young, non-Trinidadian islanders and African Americans
who now join the ranks of Brooklyn's pan playing youth.

Increased government funding for multicultural arts in the late
1980s and early 1990s also helped bolster New York's steel pan
movement. Steelbands including CASYM, the BWIA Sonatas, the
Silhouettes, and Moods Pan Groove have played for numerous music
events sponsored by colleges, museums, city parks, and arts organizations like the World Music Institute, City Lore, the Ethnic Folk
Arts Center, the Brooklyn Arts Council, and the Queens Council on
the Arts. Directly or indirectly through such arts organizations,
steelbands have received government support from the National
Endowment for the Arts, the New York State Council on the Arts,
and the New York City Department of Cultural Affairs. In the context of the multicultural arts movement, pan is presented as a unique
Trinidadian art form that West Indians can be proud of and others
can appreciate. Moreover, these new performance opportunities may
explain why younger pan players feel less resentful than their elders about pan's loss of prominence in the Eastern Parkway Carnival and at West Indian fetes.[5]

While pan orchestras are becoming increasingly scarce on Eastern Parkway, the WIADCA's Panorama contest continues to attract
considerable attention. Particularly impressive is Despers USA, a
Brooklyn-based band that has won the competition in 1993, 1994,
1995, 1996, and 1997, each year surpassing approximately a dozen
other contestants. Like many bands, the membership of Despers
swells to between fifty and sixty players for Carnival Panorama,
and then decreases to a core of fifteen to twenty who maintain a
broad repertory of material for year-round performances at parties, concerts and festivals.

The recent establishment and growth of a Carnival J'Ouvert celebration in central Brooklyn is another indication of pan's rejuve-
nation. In Port of Spain, J'Ouvert (*Jour Ouvert*—"break of day")
marks the opening of Trinidad's Carnival with predawn revelry featuring steelband music, old mas costuming, and high-spirited dancing (Stuempfle 1995, 203-205). While deejays and sound systems
have gradually come to dominate the daytime Carnival festivities,
steelbands remain a major source of music for the early morning
J'Ouvert celebration.

J'Ouvert was not part of the original Brooklyn Labor Day Carnival, but apparently the decline of steelband participation on the
Parkway and at fetes stirred a desire for new performance opportunities during the Carnival season. In the early hours of a Labor Day

morning, some time in the mid-1980s, members of the Pan Rebels Steel Orchestra ventured out from their panyard on Woodruff Street near Flatbush Avenue in central Brooklyn and began playing on the sidewalk, attracting a crowd of all-night party goers. The performance was repeated the next year, and turned into a boisterous block party. In following years, other bands including the Metro Steel Orchestra began showing up, as did mas bands like the Juju Jammers. Earl King, one of the organizers of these early J'Ouvert events, recalls that one Labor Day morning around three a.m., some time in the late 1980s, the bands began to spontaneously move up Bedford Avenue to Empire Boulevard and down New York Avenue, surrounded by Carnival dancers. "There were no sound systems, no deejays, just pure pan and old mas bands" he recalls, "and the people really loved it!" (King 1996).

As the impromptu J'Ouvert celebration grew in size, King and leaders of the steelbands realized they would need to create a more formal structure to avoid conflict with the authorities. In 1993 he founded J'Ouvert City International, a not-for-profit organization meant to coordinate the J'Ouvert event. With the assistance of local politicians and the police, the organization was granted permission to parade up Flatbush Avenue, across Empire Boulevard, and down Nostrand Avenue to Linden Boulevard, beginning at three o'clock on Labor Day morning (King, 1996).

To date the new J'Ouvert celebration has been enthusiastically embraced by steelbands, mas bands, and West Indian Carnival-goers alike. The 1995 event, according to King, included twelve steelbands and attracted a crowd estimated by the police to exceed 30,000. The 1996 celebration featured sixteen steelbands and a crowd estimated at 50-60,000. The 1996 route included two competition points—Mike's Diner on Flatbush Avenue, and Allan's Bakery on Nostrand Avenue—where judges awarded prizes to the steelband performing the best calypso and the best "bomb" (non-calypso tune with a calypso rhythm). The winning bands received small cash prizes, but there were no regular appearance fees. The bands came primarily for the opportunity to perform and to offer their family and friends the opportunity to "play mas" to live pan, rather than canned deejay music.[6] "J'Ouvert puts pan in the spotlight," reflects Earl King:

> You see, pan got lost on the parkway when the big sound systems and deejays took over. So we were determined to do something to preserve pan, to let our children know where Carnival really comes from. So in J'Ouvert it's just pan and

mas bands, no deejays invited. Now people are remembering the joy you can get by taking your time and playing mas with a steelband, just inching up the road, pushing pan. We're trying to revive that whole thing (King 1996).

Steel Pan and Cultural Identity in New York

Just as steel pan music is promoted as a national art in Trinidad (Stuempfle 1995, 76-124; Hill 1972), it is hailed as a cultural symbol by many leaders of New York's Trinidadian community. Like other transplanted vernacular arts, steel pan music in New York functions as a source of pride and nostalgia for immigrants in a new land. When Trinidadian New Yorkers attend Labor Day Carnival events and listen to steel pan music, they are reminded of the pleasures of their island home. When their children join a pan orchestra, both generations experience a deep sense of cultural continuity.

It would be a mistake, however, to interpret New York's steel pan movement as a quaint folk practice, disconnected from old-country origins and kept alive by aging immigrants fond of romanticizing their heritage. Steel pan is a relatively new art form, one that came into its own precisely at the time when Trinidadian immigration burgeoned. The Trinidadians who established pan in New York—Rudy King, Ellie Mannette, and Caldera Caraballo—came with dreams of carving out careers as musicians. Those who were deeply involved in the Carnival world traveled between the United States and Trinidad regularly, taking part in New York and Port of Spain festivities. Today, top players and arrangers from Trinidad like Len "Boogsie" Sharpe, Ken "Professor" Philmore, Robert Greenidge, and Clive Bradley often work with Brooklyn bands. Groups of panists, mas costume makers, and devotees move in an international Carnival circuit that includes annual celebrations in Toronto, Miami, and London, as well as those in Port of Spain and Brooklyn. Viewed from this transnational perspective, New York's steel pan movement is a vibrant extension, rather than an antiquated survival, of an ongoing Trinidad tradition.[7]

While steel pan has been embraced by many Trinidadian New Yorkers as a symbol of shared identity and community, the music itself never developed in a strictly insular, "ethnic" context. Pan players and their promoters were ready, indeed eager, to use the instrument to cross cultural boundaries in significant ways. New York's earliest panmen quickly discovered that white Americans were interested in their music. In spite of the dull repertoire requirements, playing at white clubs and parties provided much needed economic support for New York's early steelbands. Moreover, performing for white audiences in Broadway theaters, Village clubs, and prestigious concert venues like Carnegie Hall provided a degree of cultural validation for pan players who were still trying to counter pan's lingering image as crude street art. Trinidadians were fiercely proud that they had invented the steel pan by transforming discarded metal containers into sophisticated melodic instruments. They welcomed the opportunity to demonstrate, before American audiences of all backgrounds, their instrument's capabilities of playing not only calypso, but also American jazz and popular music and European classics. In more recent years, the multicultural arts movement has provided panmen and panwomen the opportunity to showcase their instrument and music to broader public audiences at schools, colleges, museums, and outdoor festivals.

Non-Trinidadian Caribbean people and black Americans also became involved with steel pan music in New York. Early on, a handful of West Indians from other English-speaking islands including Barbados, Grenada, and the Bahamas joined steelbands. In Harlem a number of black Americans became members of McCarthy's Harlem All Stars. Today the Brooklyn bands remain overwhelmingly Trinidadian in personnel, but a growing number of Jamaican, Haitian, Latino, and black American youth are joining school and community center-based bands. This increased diversity has not, to date, posed a serious threat to New York's Trinidadian players, who seem to welcome the trend. For them the pan's ability to attract non-Trinidadian players, to produce non-Trinidadian music, and to entertain non-Trinidadian audiences simply underscores the instrument's exceptional qualities and potential widespread appeal.

While New York's steel pan players have, by nature and necessity, broadened their repertoires and audience base, they have never lost touch with their primary Trinidadian constituents. The Labor Day Panorama event still attracts an audience that is primarily West Indian, and heavily Trinidadian in makeup. While some lament the decline of pan's presence on Eastern Parkway, the establishment of the Trinidad-style J'Ouvert celebration, with its emphasis on steel pan music and old mas costuming, appears to be a reassertion of Trinidadian tradition. Pan players agree that their bands achieve peak performances when playing a well-arranged calypso for an appreciative Trinidadian audience in a competitive Carnival setting.

Younger Trinidadian-American panmen and panwomen, particularly those born in New York, are somewhat ambivalent when it comes to questions of music and cultural identity. On the one hand, they are well aware of the steel pan's Trinidadian origins, and are proud that other Americans—black, white, Latino, or Caribbean immigrants of non-Trinidadian origin—are interested in listening to and playing their instrument. Yet according to Arddin Herbert—the twenty-seven year old, Trinidadian-born leader of Brooklyn's CASYM Steel Orchestra—most of the young players he instructs are more concerned with musical creativity than with ethnic identity. For them the steel pan is a means to express their eclectic musical tastes, which range from Caribbean soca, reggae, zouk, and salsa to American jazz, pop and hip hop. Herbert's goal is "to create a steel orchestra that can play many musical styles for any audience in any situation" (Herbert 1997). His players move comfortably between street and stage, from a J'Ouvert Carnival procession to a college concert hall. These young panmen and panwomen demonstrate great resourcefulness and continue to embrace the "open and inclusive" musical sensibility that Steve Stuempfle (1995, 219-220) argues has characterized the steelband movement in Trinidad since its inception. A willingness to draw on diverse musical influences, to seek new performance settings within, as well as outside, their Trinidadian community, and to develop alternative funding sources will be necessary for this new generation of pan players to maintain their craft in an increasingly multicultural, competitive, global center like New York City.

NOTES

1. We approach the study of urban music cultures from a transcultural, interactive perspective as outlined by Glasser (1995, 1-12) in her work on Puerto Rican music in New York. See also her contribution to this volume. The works of Manuel (1988; 16-23), Coplan (1982; 1985), and Waterman (1990) have informed our thinking regarding the role of urban popular music styles in negotiating group identity and in mediating tensions across cultural boundaries. See also Allen (1991, 205-227) for a case study of African-American music style and social identity in New York City.

2. *Wiltwyck Steel Band Under the Direction of Kim Loy Wong,* Folkway Records FS 3834, 1959; *The Steel Drums of Kim Loy Wong,* Folkway Records FI 8367, 1961.

3. *Steelband Spectacular: The Sound of the Caribbean with the Sunjet Serenaders Steelband,* Columbia Records CS 9260, 1966. The

album notes brim with romantic descriptions of the Caribbean and steelband music, but offer no information on the Sunjet Serenaders, and make no mention that the band is from Brooklyn. The album cover features an image of the orchestra playing on a sparkling beach, apparently somewhere in the Caribbean. The photograph, however, was actually taken at Jones Beach, Long Island. Although the recording featured mostly American songs, Columbia sought to promote the Sunjets as "authentic" West Indian performers, and purposely hid the band's Brooklyn affiliation.

4. See the following reviews of the Lenox Avenue Carnival in the *New York Amsterdam News*: 8 September 1951, p.1 and p.19; 12 September 1953, p.1; 10 September 1955, p.1; 7 September 1957, p.2; and 12 September 1959, p.1.

5. Arddin Herbert (1997), leader of the CASYM Steel Orchestra, claims that his young pan players show little interest in having their orchestra take part in the Eastern Parkway Carnival parade. Carnival is no longer the group's central focus, as it plays year-round at public schools, colleges, and arts festivals. The CASYM orchestra does compete in the Saturday evening Carnival Panorama and participates in the Monday morning J'Ouvert festivities, but on Labor Day afternoon its members prefer to don costumes and jump up with their own mas bands on Eastern Parkway.

6. The description of the 1996 J'Ouvert celebration is based on the co-authors' personal observations of the event.

7. The international dimension of New York City's steelband movement supports recent arguments (Austerlitz 1997, 123-134; Glasser 1995, 1-12; Manuel 1995, 241-243) that contemporary immigrant music cultures, particularly those of the Caribbean diaspora, must be understood as components of transnational circuits rather than as isolated transplants of old country tradition.

REFERENCES CITED

Allen, Ray. 1991. *Singing in the Spirit: African-American Sacred Quartets in New York City*. Philadelphia: University of Pennsylvania Press.

Austerlitz, Paul. 1997. *Merengue Dominican Music and Identity.* Philadelphia: Temple University Press.

Caraballo, Reynolds "Caldera." 29 July 1996. Personal interview by authors.

Coplan, David. 1982. "The Urbanization of African Music: Some Theoretical Observations." *Popular Music* 2: 113-130.

_____. 1985. *In Township Tonight: South Africa's Black City Music and Theatre.* London: Longman Press.

Glasser, Ruth. 1995. *My Music Is My Flag: Puerto Rican Musicians and Their New York Communities, 1917-1940.* Berkeley: University of California Press.

Herbert, Arddin. 23 July 1997. Personal interview by authors.

Henry, Clyde. 24 September 1996. Phone interview by authors.

Hill, Donald. 1994. "A History of West Indian Carnival in New York City to 1978." *New York Folklore* 20 (Winter Spring): 47- 66.

Hill, Errol. 1972. *The Trinidad Carnival: Mandate for a National Theater.* Austin: University of Texas Press.

Kasinitz, Philip. 1992. *Caribbean New York: Black Immigrants and the Politics of Race.* Ithaca: Cornell University Press.

King, Earl. 9 September 1996. Phone interview by authors.

King, Rudy. 25 October 1995. Personal interview by authors.

Mannette, Ellie. October 1968. Personal interview with co-author Les Slater.

Manuel, Peter. 1988. *Popular Musics of the Non-Western World.* New York: Oxford University Press.

Manuel, Peter, with Kenneth Bilby and Michael Largey. 1995. *Caribbean Currents: Caribbean Music from Rumba to Reggae.* Philadelphia: Temple University Press.

Mauge, Conrad. 25 July 1996. Personal interview by authors.

Monroe, Winston. 8 August 1996. Personal interview by authors.

Morancie, Horace. 7 July 1996. Personal interview by authors.

Slater, Les. 1996. "The Evolution of Steelband: An Ongoing Quest for Respectability." In *Music of the Caribbean*, ed. Beverley Anderson, 109-119. New York: McGraw Hill.

Stuempfle, Stephen. 1995. *The Steelband Movement: The Forging of a National Art in Trinidad and Tobago.* Philadelphia: University of Pennsylvania Press.

Waterman, Christopher. 1990. *Juju: A Socal History and Ethnography of an African Popular Music.* Chicago: University of Chicago Press.

West Indian American Day Carnival Association, Brooklyn, NY.
   1974. Carnival Program Book.
   1975. Carnival Program Book.
   1976. Carnival Program Book.
   1977. Carnival Program Book.
Wong, Kim Loy. 1965. Personal conversations with co-author Les
   Slater.

Moving the Big Apple
Tabou Combo's Diasporic Dreams[1]

Gage Averill

The story with the diaspora is that a guy is living far from his
country, far from all his habits, his family, his music, his foods,
all those things that he's used to. He's living in a place where
things are totally different. The way of living is completely
upside down for him. He's not used to the winter or living like
a number. He's used to a very warm way of living. He's coming from a small town where everybody knows everybody,
going to a subway in a big city where nobody knows anybody.
That's very hard for him. That's why the music of groups like
Tabou has such an appeal for him.
                    Bobby Denis (1988), Haitian recording engineer

For nearly thirty years, Tabou Combo has been in the trenches of
Haitian music, a standard-bearer for Haitian *konpa* in the
non-Haitian market with thirty albums to its credit. The story of
this band, which Ralph Boncy has called "Haiti's Rolling Stones,"[2]
encompasses, reflects, and in some ways has helped to shape the
history of Haitian music of the last three decades. My decision to
focus on a single band, to delve into musical portraiture, was a choice
to dispense with the conceit that a single article could somehow
represent the music of the New York Haitian diaspora.[3] What follows instead is a qualitative study, largely from the musicians' points
of view, of an immigrant band's history and musical praxis. Examining the group's musical choices helps illuminate what it means to
be based in the diaspora (and particularly in New York City) and
how this has affected the musicians' relationship to their constituents. More specifically, this is a study in audience development—

that aspect of musical praxis dedicated to cultivating a network of commercial patronage and to capturing market position. To accomplish these goals, a band such as Tabou Combo continually analyzes its existing and potential listeners, refines a distinctive style and repertory expressed in concert performances and recordings, and employs the commercial and media promotional tools at its disposal to further its reputation. Tabou Combo offers an ideal study of audience development because the group's displacement to New York gave members access to a Haitian diasporic audience (with continued sales and tours to the insular audience) and placed them in close proximity to the largest, most demographically complex urban market in the United States as well as to a major node of the North American recording industry.

Haiti: Souvenir of Tabou Combo[4]

In the early 1960s, urban Haiti was experiencing its own chapter in the worldwide explosion of youth subculture. School-age, middle-class youth were eager to display generational differences and to enjoy their adolescence at school parties, cinema-concerts, church *kèmès-s* (Sunday or early evening bazaars), and volleyball and soccer games. Haiti's aspiring rock 'n' rollers took a cue from the light French rocker Johnny Halladay, calling their music *yeye* (originally from the Beatles' refrain "Yeah, Yeah, Yeah" in "She Loves You"). Haitian yeye groups readily appropriated Elvis Presley, the twist, and the Beatles in addition to French rock, creating bands with "tough" male-bonding names such as Les Copains (The Buddies), Les Aces de Pétion-Ville (The Aces of Pétion-Ville), Les Blousons Noirs (Black Shirts, after the "Teddy Boy" movement of British teenagers), Les Shelberts (The Show-offs), and Les Loups Noirs (The Black Wolves). Many of the students who formed the backbone of the yeye movement were only fourteen to seventeen years old in the years 1962-67 and hailed from the upper-class suburb of Port-au-Prince called Pétion-Ville, approximately five kilometers— or a twenty minute drive—up into the hills from the capital.

The yeye groups employed a rock-like instrumentation (electric guitars and bass, drum set, and often saxophone) and a largely imported repertory. The shift to more local musics had its roots in the increased isolation of Haiti coupled with the fervent nationalistic (sometimes xenophobic) ideology of the Duvalier dictatorship, as well as to the desire of school students to dance to the straightforward *compas-direct* (spelled *konpa* in Creole) rhythm, the popular Haitian dance that had been developed a decade earlier by saxophonist Nemours Jean-Baptiste. Whereas most rock dances did not involve bodily contact, konpa was an intimate couples dance. To play konpa properly, yeye bands added a conga and a combination of bell and tamtam (floor tom drum), as these were instruments that had come to define a distinctive konpa groove. Deejay Rico Jean-Baptiste coined the name "mini-djaz" to describe these ensembles—"mini" in reference to their small size, and "djaz," a Creole term synonymous for "dance band." Early stars of the new movement included Ibo Combo, Shleu Shleu, Les Ambassadeurs, Les Fantaisistes de Carrefour, Les Difficiles de Pétion-Ville, and, of course, Tabou Combo.

In 1967, after the school day ended at the Lycée (high school) François Duvalier, Albert Chancy, and his friend Herman Nau often played music together in a small storefront gallery with Nau using a table as a drum.[5] After finding an electric bass, borrowing an amplifier, and recruiting a violinist and two vocalists, the young men named themselves Los Incognitos de Pétion-Ville.[6] They added a rhythm guitar and accordion for their first public performance. Their early repertory was eclectic, and included light classical waltzes, boleros, tangos, bossa novas, and konpa.

Members of the band used to gather at the house of guitarist Alix "Tit" Pascal, a leader of the band Ibo Combo and one of the most sophisticated jazz musicians in the country. Pascal had been recently shot by a Tonton Makout and was paralyzed from the waist down, but these sessions with him were the start of his long influence on the band. By 1968, Herman Nau had purchased a drum set and proceeded to help define konpa set drumming with his emphasis on bass drum downbeats and the ride cymbal to play the *kata*, a pattern borrowed from Haitian *Vodou* and *Rara* percussion traditions. Under Nau, the drum set took its place as the third leg of the konpa rhythm section.[7]

Following a debut concert at the Church of Saint Pierre in Pétion-Ville, the group went on to play at baptisms, communions, and confirmation parties. The members were dissatisfied with the Spanish name "Los Incognitos" and wanted to be, as Joseph put it, "more nationalistic, more Haitian with the name." In its place Albert Chancy selected "Tabou" (the French spelling of "taboo," from the Tongan word for "marked as sacred, prohibited from use"), the name of a local flower store. The use of the term "combo" was a tribute to Ibo Combo, Pascal's ensemble whose jazzy konpa and bossa nova had influenced young musicians in Pétion-Ville. (Ibo Combo used the "combo" label to link itself to American and Brazilian combo jazz and bossa nova groups.) It is striking that the name Tabou

Combo, standing for a band that has always aggressively hybridized local and global expressions, has such global reach, even while conceived within a framework of assertive local identity.

Foregoing a lead saxophone (in contrast to Shleu-Shleu and many other mini-djaz-s), Tabou Combo became the only mini-djaz to feature an accordionist and, like Les Difficiles de Pétion-Ville, emphasize guitars. Many of Haiti's most influential guitarists including Jean-Claude Jean, Dadou Pasquet, Elysée Pyronneau, Robert Martino, and Claude Marcelin came out of these two groups or their spin-offs. Although Tabou Combo was influenced by the Rolling Stones, the Beatles, James Brown, and Sly and the Family Stone, its early repertory leaned more toward Latin pieces than Euro-American, and its first album featured two boleros and a bossa nova ("Carole") among a number of konpa songs.

Tabou Combo played at local dances, theaters, and eventually on Tele-Haïti. In 1969 the ensemble won the Radio d'Haïti prize for best group of the year, and recorded a best-selling debut album, *Haïti* (Ibo Records ILP-146, 1969), for Joe Anson's Ibo Records.[8] After the release of the album, Albert Chancy's parents sent him abroad to pursue journalism at a Canadian university. Given Albert's leadership role in the group and the divergent goals of the other musicians (for example, Adolphe "Ti Dòf" Chancy, Albert's brother, went to Puerto Rico to study administration), the group decided to disband. Its *bal adieu* (farewell party) at the famous Ibo Lélé Hotel nightclub was one of the year's major social events. The concert promoter came up with $700 to record a live final tribute album, but crowd noise drowned out the music, so recording engineer Bobby Denis re-recorded the songs three days later on the floor of another nightclub (Cabane Choucoune) during off hours. *Disque Souvenir de Tabou Combo* (Memory of Tabou Combo, no catalogue number), had a single run of 500 copies. Four of the eight songs on the album showed up on the first two Tabou Combo releases in the United States.

In three short years Tabou Combo had become Haiti's most popular band, inspiring middle-class, urban youth to revitalize a musical genre (konpa) identified with the 1950s. Tabou Combo's style of konpa was thus positioned to become the music of nostalgic consumption in New York and the rest of the diaspora.

At the Canne à Sucre: Respect!

Herman Nau, Serge Guerrier, Jean-Claude Jean, and Yvon "Kapi" André made their way to New York City to work and attend school.

New York already had the second-largest concentration of Haitians in the world after the capital city of Port-au-Prince, but had only one band of any stature (Original Shleu Shleu) to play for the increasingly well-off and nostalgic community. Much of the Haitian "colony"—as it was called by Haitians—consisted of upper-class political refugees from Papa Doc's terror, although a younger generation of middle-class refugees, fleeing both political repression and economic despair, made up a growing segment of the community.

Joined by Haitian emigrants including sixteen-year-old guitarist Dadou Pasquet and conga player Weston Etienne, Tabou Combo began practicing in November of 1970 in a Brooklyn basement. When the group played its first event at a party on Roosevelt Avenue in Queens it was clear that an audience existed for the band. "Kapi" André recalls:

> We didn't play regularly because the group wasn't solid. We practiced and practiced and in February of 1971, we called "Fanfan" from Chicago (where he was studying and working and trying to pursue a soccer career) and he came to New York. "Shoubou" [Roger M. Etienne] came from Haiti, and bassist "Ti-Dòf" (Adolphe Chancy) eventually came up from Puerto Rico. As the original members came, some of the ones who had replaced them were out. We began like that. By the summer of 1971, we were playing at the Canne à Sucre (André 1989).

Starting in the late 1960s, a part-time Haitian nightclub called Club Camaraderie (named after an exclusive club in Haiti) opened on certain nights in a Chinese Restaurant called the Shin-Shin Palace. Brooklyn's first full-time Haitian restaurant/nightclub, however, was the Canne à Sucre (Sugar Cane). Tabou used the club as a home base for a short while, and as the recording site for its first United States album, *Tabou Combo à la Canne à Sucre* (Rotel Records, 1971). The album's cover shows the group sporting afros and dressed in jeans (some in denim or leather jackets), seated around the club's modest but colorful dance floor. The songs are remarkably like those of Tabou's Haiti years despite the changes in personnel (Adolphe Chancy replaced by Yvon Ciné on bass, Albert Chancy by André "Dadou" Pasquet on guitar, and Paul Gonnel by Guery Legagneur on accordion). The lyrics were still in Creole, but some of the exclamations and dialogue appeared in English, as in this opening to the song "Manou": "Can I really get into it? Yeah! Are you ready, people? Yeah! Let's Go!"

The Canne à Sucre was soon supplanted by a host of other Brooklyn clubs such as Coconut Grove Night Club on Foster Avenue, Ka Bouki on Ocean Parkway, and Le Caribana Club near Grand Army Plaza. Soon, however, many of the more prestigious clubs were situated in Queens, where middle-class Haitian Americans (including many from elite backgrounds in Haiti) could feel more secure that they would associate only with those of their own class. The Malibu Caterers (Flushing), Le Chalet (Jamaica), Le Club Bacoulou (Cambria Heights), Olympia Palace (Queens City), and Chateau Royale Nightclub (Queens Village) were the most popular. For shows on the level of a "gala" or "spèktak" (spectacle), a promoter generally rented a local school or college such as Prospect Heights, Clara Barton, or George Wingate High Schools in Brooklyn; Andrew Jackson High School in Cambria Heights; Queens College; and Brooklyn College.

The typical gala program featured a comic serving as emcee, dance bands, folkloric dance troupes, and singers. This type of formulaic performance event had a long history in Haiti, where galas were booked at movie theaters for holidays and special occasions. Transplanted to New York, they became Haitian versions of a more widespread phenomenon, the ethnic variety show. Some of the most popular of these galas in the 1970s were the annual "Trophy Nights" at the Coconut Grove Night Club (later moved to Brooklyn College), sponsored by the Haitian American Independent Talent Inc. (H.A.I.T.I.). In 1972, the trophy for "most popular band," awarded by Marc's Records, went to Tabou Combo. High-prestige crossover venues proved irresistible to promoters of Haitian music like Earl Harris, who booked The Felt Forum at Madison Square Garden for the first time in 1974 for a Haitian gala. The show featured comedian Languichatte as emcee; singers Ansy Derose, Paulette St. Lot, and Roger Colas; the Haitian dance troupe Shango Folk Group; and dance bands Orchestre Septentrionale (Haiti), Jazz des Jeunes, and Tabou Combo. Similar events were sponsored by sporting clubs and regional associations, as in the presentation of volleyball trophies in 1974 by the Cacos Athletic Club.[9] On the bill were Orchestre Septentrionale, the Ibo Dancers folkloric troupe, a little-known player of both the accordion and saw, a Haitian tenor, and "the nail of the soirée, the unsurpassable Tabou Combo."

Tabou's fourth album, *Respect* (Mini Records MRS 1039, 1972-3), was its first release for Fred Paul's Mini Records. Up until this point, Haitian recording had been dominated by Joe Anson (Ibo Records) and Marc Duverger (Marc Records). *Respect* was Paul's first major vehicle:

When I did *Respect*, that's when I really had an impact on the
market . . . that was a big deal. It was difficult for me to make
a deal with those guys. I knew "Fanfan" from playing soccer
in Haiti. And I called "Fanfan" and they had the recording
and I told Fanfan, "Yeah, I can do a good job," and he went
along. It was a time we were just making records, we weren't
really producing, because most of these tapes were brought
from Haiti. Sometimes you had never heard the song. You're
not recording the band, you know, they're sending you the
tape and you put it on. They were doing that at Radio Haïti,
(recording engineer) Bobby Denis with the mics and so on.
And at the time, he started to come to America to do a lot of
the groups here too...at nightclubs and things like that, in
basements...live, no overdubs (Paul 1991).

By the early 1970s, even with very few groups living in New York,
the city was already the hub of the Haitian recording business. Because the New York area boasted a number of album production
facilities, it became the destination for almost all Haitian master
tapes, whether recorded in Port-au-Prince or in New York. Joe Anson
had moved to the city in the late 1950s and had operated his Ibo
Records as a transnational business out of Brooklyn with significant transactions in Port-au-Prince, where he still had family members. Marc Duverger opened up a record business out of his Brooklyn beauty shop in the mid-1960s and marketed recordings of Coupé
Cloué, Jazz des Jeunes, and Orchestre Septentrional. Rotel Records,
which produced Tabou's third album, was a production of Jessee
Markowitz (Montuno Records) and a Haitian business partner. Each
of these producers traded their records with the others to insure
distribution, and they mailed small batches to Haiti and to the
French Antilles. Interestingly, the Haitian recording business had
preceded the bands to New York.

The hybridizing and code-switching instincts so associated with
Tabou Combo are evident from the opening measures of *Respect* in
a conga evocation of a Puerto Rican *bomba* rhythm with a single-
note guitar counter-rhythm. On *Respect*, Tabou popularized the use
of introductions in disparate styles (one sounding like the Mexican
son "La Bamba," another like a Cuban *rumba*, a third with a "funky"
vocal patter in English) as a means for setting off the konpa song
section. This demonstrated the group's versatility, but it was also
intended to attract a wider African diasporic audience of other Caribbean immigrants and African Americans. On the title track, "Respect," the band outlines its encounter with diaspora audiences:

M vin antre nan Nouyòk	I came to New York City
Se moun k'ap etaje nou	People are putting us on stage
Men tout kote nou pase	Everywhere we go
Se nou menm y'ape eklame	People are praising us
Nou fin pa jwenn yon rit	We end up finding a rhythm
Ke tout satisfe tout moun...	That can satisfy everybody...
Tabou, tout danse Tabou	Tabou, everybody is dancing to Tabou[10]

Until 1974, Tabou's main competition was the band Original Shleu Shleu. However, in 1974, a second version of Shleu Shleu migrated to New York and took the name Skah Shah. The group was brought to New York by promoter George Francis to serve as competition for Tabou Combo. There is a precedent in Haitian music for pairs of ensembles to engage in heated competition (for example, Nemours Jean-Baptiste's competition with Wébert Sicot in the 1950s and 1960s), and Tabou and Skah Shah carried on this tradition in the Haitian community in New York. Joint concert appearances were often billed as "musical duels." A number of years later, the Haitian music magazine *Superstar* ran an ad for a competition between the two bands that pitted individuals of the bands against each other as in a soccer match:

> NEW! SUSPENSE! PASSION!
> Zouzoul against Fanfan Ti-Bòt,
> Herman Nau against Ti-Frè,
> Shoubou against Ti-Crane,
> Who will have the last word?
> Who will win the EQUI DISCO trophy?

Tabou's 1974 recording, *8th Sacrament* (Mini Records MRS 1044), was a milestone in the group's career. The record was licensed by Fred Paul to a French agent who in turn licensed it to Barclay Records for distribution in France. The single "New York City" peaked as No. 1 in Paris in August of 1975. The introduction to the song describes the difficulties of exile and the need to "render affection" to Haiti, but the konpa "groove" section changes subject matter and lists a long string of children's games serving as double-entendres interspersed with rapid guitar riffs and laced with exclamations in Spanish, Creole, and English. Sirens, connoting New York's raucous urban soundscape, are occasionally heard.

"New York City" was Tabou Combo's first international hit and first gold record, establishing the group's reputation in France and the French Antilles. Moreover it was the song that Tabou Combo used to announce to the world that it was a Haitian band *from New York*. Living in diaspora, poised between cultures, playing in the most ethnically diverse city in the world, group members wanted to show that they were up to the challenge of the global city and the globe. The exposure of Haitian music to a mainstream French audience was an inspiring development for Haitian musicians. Guitarist Ricardo "Ti-Plume" Franck was in Paris at the time:

> One day I was in Paris and I woke up—I was so proud to listen to the radio and hear Haitian music...it was Tabou Combo music. The music sounded to me like something so sweet! I pinched myself to see if I was awake. Tabou Combo was playing on the Radio Television Française and the band was talking about music! That was a big thing. "New York City"...and I said, maybe this is the big break for Haitian music (Franck 1993).

The band received about $10,000 in royalties from airplay because they had joined the French music association, SACEM, but they had difficulties collecting any royalties from album sales because of the multiple assignments of ownership from Fred Paul to a French agent to Barclay. On a subsequent trip to Paris to perform, some of the band members visited music industry offices attempting to collect on what they felt was owed. Conflicts erupted over musical direction, finances, and leadership. Alix Pascal recalls:

> The misunderstanding of the international show-business thing created a lot of confusion. An unexpected hit, suddenly, for guys from Haiti, from a corner of the community in Brooklyn, suddenly finding themselves on the charts. Barry White, Michael Jackson, everybody was behind us on the charts. You need preparation for that. We weren't successful yet! I told them "We've been accepted, but now we have to prove ourselves. That's the way the business works...." We were planning the future of the band, and some of the guys thought we were plotting against them. So with that chaos, everything falls apart (Pascal 1988).

From its reorganization in 1971 through its success with "New York City," Tabou Combo explored the new environment, competitively positioned itself against other Haitian bands for "market share" of the Haitian diasporic audience, and incorporated diverse musical materials—most reflecting the varied musical soundscape of New York City—into its konpa. The taste of a new level of success, however, made the band hungry to move aggressively into expanded markets.

The (Indestructible) Masters, Moving the Big Apple

The Masters was conceived as a follow-up album (also on Mini Records and licensed for distribution in France) to capitalize on the success of "New York City," and some of the wrangling over musical direction helped the album to achieve a creative and experimental, if not economic, success. Ralph Boncy called the album, "the most ambitious, the densest and the most astounding of Tabou" (Boncy 1992, 99). On the cover, the band posed in academic regalia on the lawn at Queens College. A minor hit in Spanish called "Inflacion" (to the tune of one of their Haiti-era hits, "Toyota") began with an introduction in a traditional Vodou rhythm called *mayi*.[11]

When *The Masters* fell short of the previous recording's international success, the band entered a period of recriminations and reorganization. Subgroups consolidated and a mood of suspicion and jealousy hung over the members. Whereas band members had felt disappointed by their inability to collect royalties on their hit record, they at least believed that "New York City" had developed an ardent following in far-flung places. But following Tabou Combo's failure to recapture that market, members began to see "New York City" as a song that had been consumed in France and elsewhere as a novelty item, as a flavor-of-the-month hit rather than a serious market inroad. Dadou Pasquet, who had become one of the most visible and popular musicians in the group, left to form Magnum Band with his brother, Tico. Dadou had been accused of relying too strongly on technical virtuosity and on developing a "cult of personality" in conflict with the expressed collectivist ideal of the band. Whereas other major Haitian bands had already undergone schisms of this sort (Shleu Shleu to Skah Shah, Les Difficiles to D. P. Express, and D. P. Express to Gypsies), this was the first major rift in "The Brothers Tabou." When Pasquet left, Elysée Pyronneau took his place as lead guitarist. From the north of Haiti and largely self-taught, Pyronneau was nonetheless musically talented and was soon recognized as an arranging "maestro" of the group.

The remaining original members plus Pyronneau regrouped and came out with *Indestructible* (Mini Records, 1976), signaling to their fans that Tabou Combo considered itself indestructible and not dependent on individuals. The following year, 1977, they released a tenth-year commemorative album called *L'An X* (Year Ten) on Rotel Records. This was a year of great changes for the group, especially in instrumentation. The accordion was dropped from their line-up (more by chance than by design, although many felt that its sound had become antiquated). At about the same time an American trumpet player, Rob Little, and an African-American trombonist, Andrew "Dr. Black" Washington were added. Behind this change was a growing orientation toward an African-American funk and soul market, which Tabou members thought they could crack. They had in mind a Caribbean-flavored version of The Commodores; Earth, Wind, and Fire; Tower of Power; and Parliament-Funkadelic, all of which featured collective vocal choruses on top of funky rhythm tracks interspersed with powerful horn lines. With the new fad requiring a full horn section (trombone, saxophones, and trumpets), the use of non-Haitian horn players became a staple of Haitian bands. The foreigners, however, never made it to the inner circles of the Haitian bands, instead always working as contract or "gig" musicians for a paycheck. *L'An X* was the first Tabou album to be dominated by crossover aesthetics. Much of the album was devoted to disco and funk: "Let Me Play That Funky Music," "Let's Do the Groove," "Tabou Disco," and "Hoola Hoop Disco." The band, especially Adolphe Chancy, felt the time was right for "coconut funk" (funk with a tropical flavor) to join funk and soul in the African-American music market.

This crossover fever helped configure the next three album projects. *Tabou Mania* (Mini Records MRS 1070, 1978) resembled an Earth, Wind & Fire album cover. The band's costumes, designed by drummer Herman Nau, were rooted in science fiction and fantasy, the "afro-naut" look adopted by George Clinton's P-Funk and other funk bands.[12] The pyramid on the cover from which the band members were pictured emerging, however, is a Masonic symbol and was chosen precisely because a number of the band members were Freemasons. Look for the Masonic symbols floating on the backs of Tabou albums as well as for the Freemason pyramid-and-eye symbol reappropriated from the United States dollar.

In accord with market standards, Tabou stopped performing stylistically contrasting introductions to their konpa sections, a device that had become a cliché in konpa. As Jean-Yves Joseph related:

> This [old] form of the [konpa] song was very Latin—introduction, development, conclusion, coda. We don't do that anymore. We said that if the deejays start playing the music in the middle, there must be something wrong with the beginning, so now we start the beginning very hot. We used to start

the introduction with a lot of brass or whatever, then the singer starts. They always start the [konpa rhythm] in the break. [The discotheque deejays] had a medley of Tabou Combo's music and what they did was they put the songs together from every break. The breaks were always there and we did that on purpose so they could mix it that way. And we were very hot in discos because we had these breaks that were easy to mix (Joseph 1989).

The Music Machine album produced one of Tabou Combo's biggest hits, "Mabouya," and marked a resurgence of the band, now with the nickname "Superstars." A version of the dance groove from the previously recorded songs "Respect" and "Respect/Zapaton," "Mabouya" was very successful in the Caribbean and in parts of South and Central America.[13] Hoping to maintain the focus on the African-American market, the album also featured a disco number, "Let's Dance Disco," and a fusion piece in Creole and English, "Light Is Coming Your Way." Tabou Combo's last collaboration with Mini Records for many years was a twelve-inch maxi-single called "Island Women" sung in English by "Fanfan" Joseph on one side and in Creole by "Shoubou" Eugène on the reverse. Like "Inflacion," this was an effort to seek out a new audience through linguistic code switching. Following success in Panama with "Mabouya" (which was sung there informally with obscene cognate lyrics in Spanish), Tabou Combo recorded "Panama Querida" in Spanish as a tribute.

In another gesture to the African-American market, Tabou Combo adopted a logo based on the neo-Gothic, metallic relief logo of The Commodores. In 1976-77, Tabou Combo started working with the American recording engineer James Farber to prepare a demo (*Moving the Big Apple*, unreleased) for Benny Ashburn, the manager of The Commodores. Allen Bailey, a friend of Lionel Richie and a Manhattan talent agent, introduced Ashburn to the group, which was hoping to score a recording contract with Motown Records. When this fell through, cynicism about the music industry deepened to the point that the band resolved to set out alone. The group founded Tabou Combo Records and Tapes (distributed by Adolphe Chancy's Chancy Records and Tapes), the Tabou Combo Fan Club, the Tabou Combo Entertainment Corporation, and Tabou Combo Publishing/ASCAP. This was an effort to take control of its public image and reputation and to control the copyright profit stream by cutting out the middlemen. Chancy, who led the business side of the band, also opened a record outlet, Chancy's Records, in Brooklyn.

The Brooklyn Bridge serves as the setting for the portrait of the six original members of Tabou Combo (plus one) in 1982. From left to right are: Elysée Pyronneau, Jean-Yves "Fanfan Ti-Bòt" Joseph, Herman Nau, Jean-Claude "Coq" Jean, Yvon "Kapi" André, Roger "Shoubou" Eugène, Adolphe "Ti-Dòf" Chancy. From the cover to the album Ce Konsa Ce Konsa, *Chancy Records and Tapes TCLP 8015. Photo by Everald Alcindor.*

"Voye Monte," the title track of Tabou Combo's first self-produced album (*Voye Monte* TCLP 7975, 1979) was a moderate hit, while "Baissez-Bas" ("Get Down Low"), from the next album (*Baissez-Bas* TCLP 7985, 1980), sold in the vicinity of 60,000 copies. Tabou Combo also gave credit to the initiator of konpa on the same album with the song "Hommage à Nemours Jean-Baptiste," which argued that Nemours' konpa rhythm was a great Haitian cultural heritage:

Li pa ban nou travay	He didn't give us work
Li pa ban nou lajan	He didn't give us money
Men li ban nou konpa	But he gave us the konpa
Ala bèl eritay-sa	What a beautiful heritage!
Nemours Jean-Baptiste	Nemours Jean-Baptiste
Fòk nou kapab mete tèt	
ansanm	We have to put our heads together
Pou nou kab venere w	To venerate you
Tankou Lewòp venere	
Moza	Like Europe venerates Mozart [14]

Many such nostalgic tributes originated in the diaspora, which was already infused with a patriotic longing for Haiti. Tabou Combo's next album, *Ce Konsa Ce Konsa* (TCLP 8015, 1982-83), carved out new territory for the band with socially relevant or *angaje* pieces by Jean-Yves Joseph ("Préjugé"/"Prejudice") and Yvon André ("Partagé"/ "Share," aimed at the wealthy and powerful). Joseph's "Préjugé" asked: "Eske gen yon lwa de lanati ki di ke lè w nwa, fòk ou pase mizè?" ("Is there a law of nature that says that if you are black, you have to live in poverty?"). Tabou Combo had also taken note of the *angaje* dance music of Ti-Manno's D. P. Express in Haiti. The two groups had performed together in a 1979 Dominican fundraiser for victims of Hurricane David, right at the peak of D. P. Express's popularity (Ti-Manno wrote his hit "David" about the Hurricane). This was the start of a period in which the government of Baby Doc Duvalier began to unravel under a series of crises. In part as a result, Tabou Combo joined a number of other bands in issuing songs with heightened social consciousness, although this was never a primary focus for the group.

Throughout the early 1980s, Tabou Combo travelled each year to perform in Haiti where the musicians were greeted as superstars of the first order. Very few musicians who had established themselves in the diaspora in the 1970s moved back for very long to Haiti. Most were doing better economically than their counterparts in Haiti, and the atmosphere in Haiti in the early 1980s was one of economic decline and growing social unrest. Tours to Haiti, however, were regarded as essential to preserving a broad transnational Haitian audience. At a concert at Ibo Beach in 1982 and at an elaborate show at the plaza in Pétion-Ville in 1983, Tabou Combo regaled the crowds with splashy stage presentations, space-age costumes, a four-person North American horn section, and a hard rocking brand of konpa laced with raps and audible traces of African-American disco and funk. These diverse stylistic influences, derived in part from Tabou Combo's location in the diaspora, did not necessarily divide it from an insular Haitian audience, but rather contributed to the band's popularity in Haiti where it was widely imitated. In this way, popular music aesthetics were negotiated across the insular-diasporic barrier, helping to construct transnational communities-of-taste.

In the decade following "New York City," Tabou Combo had embarked on an ambitious journey to colonize African-American markets while maintaining its pre-eminence in Haitian diasporic and insular markets and its popularity in the French Antilles. To accomplish this, Tabou Combo reconfigured its sound in the direction of funk and disco, while dropping its predilection for stylistically diverse introductions in favor of a broader repertory. Key to the band's stylistic praxis was this need to continually reinvent itself to keep up with changing musical tastes. As a result of its contractual difficulties with both Haitian and non-Haitian producers and record companies, Tabou Combo pioneered an in-house production and promotion strategy designed to maintain a steady income stream from copyrights on their compositions.

Stay Out of My Business

In the mid-1980s, Tabou Combo began to encounter strong competition from the Paris-based Antillean group Kassav, not only in the Antillean market but increasingly in the Haitian market as well. Kassav, led by studio musicians Jacob Desvarieux and Georges Décimus, had been modeled in part on Tabou Combo. The band's technologically refined and catchy "zouk" was an outgrowth of Haitian konpa and *kadans*.[15] Beginning with the Haitian-based group Zèklè and continuing with other young Haitian groups or individuals like Skandal, Emeline Michèl, Zin, and the Phantoms, a younger generation of players (calling themselves the *nouvèl jenerasyon*) was emerging to compete with Kassav and the older Haitian bands with a youthful, cosmopolitan, and technological sound. At the same time, a roots music (*mizik rasin*) movement, in part inspired by Bob Marley and Rastafarians in Jamaica, surged in popularity, led by Boukman Eksperyans, Samba Yo, Foula, Boukan Ginen, and Rara Machine. Although this movement mixed international pop with Vodou percussion and with Afro-Haitian spiritual and political themes, its most popular tunes were the topical, Rara-style songs associated with Carnival. In the heady atmosphere of change and revolution following the 1986 ouster of the Duvaliers from Haiti, both these Haitian musical movements viewed themselves not just as alternatives to konpa but as successors to it. "King Kino" of the nouvèl jenerasyon group Phantoms directed some particularly pointed remarks at Tabou Combo:

> Many musical groups would like to constantly occupy the front stage, but they don't deserve this honor. As for me, I say, "To each their time." The change that we have realized in Phantoms should be implemented at all levels. We encourage musicians from all generations to participate in the struggle to liberate Haiti. I would like to ask my friends in Tabou what they have done for their country or for the Haitian people in these difficult moments. I reject the idea that a musician shouldn't engage in politics...no one can pretend that they're neutral. One goes down one route or the other (Rainer 1994, 18).

Thus, the members of Tabou Combo found themselves in danger of becoming increasingly irrelevant in the face of political changes in Haiti and the desertion of segments of their audience (especially younger Haitians) in favor of zouk, nouvèl jenerasyon, mizik rasin, and African-American hip hop. Albums released after 1986 can be viewed in part as responses to these challenges, as Tabou Combo restructured its musical formula to incorporate innovations found in these new Haitian and African-American styles. For the 1987-88 album *Kitem Fe Zafem* ("Stay Out of My Business,") the group enlisted keyboard player Ernst Marcelin, who supplanted some of the texture formerly supplied by the two guitars with synthesizers. They chipped away at the continuous "wall-of-sound" approach that had characterized much of konpa for the previous twenty years. Jean-Yves Joseph talked about the conflicts involved in the studio-based aesthetic:

> We're using less of our musicianship, relying more on the one guy playing the computer, telling him your ideas. I can even say that I'm bored now in the studio, you know, saying, "Why don't we program the whole damn thing!" It's sad, isn't it, but I don't feel so left out because I write music...but I can see a musician who doesn't write songs and he's just a musician, and he's completely left out because we're programming the cloche (bell) (Joseph 1989).

Tabou Combo recorded a song that directly spoke to proponents of the "new generation" music:

Kolonizasyon lage n pasipala	Colonialism spread us here and there
Nou dekonekte kote nou pase	Cut off from our past
Men nou gen yon fason pou nou kominike	But we have a way of communicating
Lè tanbou frape tout moun viv vre	When the drum beats everybody comes alive
Konpa tonbe? Non! Non!	Will the konpa fall? No, no!
Konpa tonbe? Nogodo!	Will the konpa fall? Nogodo
Atansyon, atansyon, Nouvèl Jenerasyon	Watch out, New Generation
Pa kite konpa ale san nou pa ranmasel	Don't let go of the konpa without picking it up[16]

The band also attempted to outdo their mizik rasin competition with a version of the venerable Rara song "Kote Moun Yo?" ("Where Are the People?"), first popularized by Jazz des Jeunes in the 1950s. In the years that followed, each Tabou Combo album contained one Rara-influenced song. In the title song to the 1993 album *Go Tabou Go* (MRS 2568), the group again acknowledged the market power of mizik rasin, suggesting that proponents of konpa and roots music should be engaging each other in dialogue rather than polarizing into hostile camps:

Rasin pa mele ak konpa, wo!	Roots music and konpa don't mingle!
Se dilere-wo!	That's a shame!
Sa ki pa konnen nou	Those who don't know us
Pa gen respè pou nou	Can't respect us[17]

Despite their loss of market share to Kassav and to the nouvèl jenerasyon, Tabou Combo continued to make impressive inroads to non-Haitian audiences, drawing an audience of over 10,000 to its concert in Central Park and playing at the New Orleans Jazz and Heritage Festival before 10,000 people. In 1990-91, *Aux Antilles* was the best-selling album in the French Antilles, and the band travelled to Paris to play at the well-known nightclub, the Zénith, using the occasion to record a double album and video called *Live aux Zénith, Les Plus Grandes Succès* (Zafem Records LP/CD 8057, 1989). Tabou Combo also toured Japan. *Zap Zap* (Zafem Records 8058) celebrated the trip and featured front and back cover photos taken at the Fujitsu Caribbean Festival. The band sang "Japonè-yo mande kisa k ape jwe la!" ("The Japanese are asking just what it is we're playing!"). Tabou Combo also inaugurated a series of concerts at SOB's, the New York crossover dance club, that eventually evolved into a regular Friday night "French Caribbean" series featuring Tabou Combo, Zin, Phantoms, System Band or other Haitian groups. All of the above venues draw from largely non-Haitian audiences of North Americans, Parisians, or Japanese, as Tabou Combo proved particularly adept at making market inroads in audiences attracted to "world beat" music in the 1990s.

In retrospect, much of Tabou Combo's third decade was devoted to countering immediate threats to the band's continued popularity: French Antillean zouk, nouvèl jenerasyon, mizik rasin, and African-American hip hop and soul. With a dash of polemic mixed with a pinch of appropriation (note that the group's 1995 album was produced by Nouvèl Jenerasyon Records), Tabou Combo has attempted to hold fast to a konpa "center" while renewing its sound with elements drawn from the band's competitors.

Conclusion

We have examined aspects of Tabou Combo's style and repertory to understand factors that have influenced the group's evolution. Many of these changes can be traced to the band's interest in "capturing" certain markets and to its competitive positioning vis-à-vis other ensembles and genres. Tabou Combo applies its own musical experiences and aesthetics while also attempting to read or imagine those of its audience (consisting of its familiar current audiences and all those audiences that the band would like to attract) in order to fashion commercially competitive songs, expressed in live concert settings and on recordings. The band also builds its reputation, a collective representation held by the public, which is created over time and amasses a certain degree of inertia or resistance to change as a result. A good reputation will augment and drive demand for the band's musical products. The goal of all of this negotiation of taste and aesthetics is precisely to increase popularity, indexed by demand for the band's creative output (expressed in concert attendance, radio play, and sales of recordings).

Tabou Combo capitalized on its New York locality to increase access to the Haitian recording and distribution business, to make connections to the North American recording business, to reach out to ethnically diverse audiences, and simply to work consistently enough to support the core group and its ancillary players for over twenty-five years. One of the most powerful features of the New York City environment for a band like Tabou Combo has been the hope that it holds out to musicians of a global audience for their music. Face to face with a microcosm of the globe that is perfectly willing to dance to their music, New York-based groups like Tabou Combo have been inspired to transcend cultural boundaries and make their diasporic dreams of global popularity a reality.

NOTES

1. Some of the material in the article appeared in my 1990 column in *The Beat* magazine (Averill 1990). I want to acknowledge my profound debt to my friend Ralph Boncy. Ralph and I considered doing an anniversary book on Tabou Combo, and we later discussed co-authoring this article. His return to Haiti from Montréal to work for a period of time made this idea impractical, but I have relied on a number of his detailed and insightful profiles of Tabou Combo hits from his book *La chanson d'Haïti, Tome 1* (1992). These include profiles of "Bébé Paramount" (pp. 29-31), "Hommage à Nemours Jean-Baptiste" (pp. 96-98), "Inflacion" (pp. 99-101), "Jalousie" (pp. 109-111), and "Junior" (pp. 121-124). I would also like to thank Jean-Yves Joseph, Ray Allen, Lois Wilcken, Yvon "Kapi" André, CC Smith, Bobby Dénis, Herman Nau, Ricardo "Ti-Plume" Franck, Alix "Tit" Pascal, André "Dadou" Pasquet, and Fred Paul.

2. Personal communication, Boncy, 1992.

3. See Laguerre (1984) for a description of the New York Haitian enclave with special attention to key cultural features (health practices, for example). Buchanan (1980) examines conflicts within the Haitian community through the prism of a single religious congregation. Schiller et al. (1987) look at the structure of community leadership and at the various political organizing strategies employed. Despite this generally excellent research, a "community" such as the Haitian community in New York City resists quantification and generalization due to factors such as its size, complexity, porous boundaries, and transitional character. Studies of musical activity in the diaspora, including my own (Averill 1995), have perhaps skewed the description of Haitian diasporic musical tastes by taking into account primarily those Haitians participating in ethnically marked cultural events. In contrast, many immigrants attend no such events and may pull out Haitian albums only on special occasions. Some Haitian-American children afraid of being labeled *jescummers* (slang for recent immigrants) or french

fries (derogatory term for French-speaking blacks) will disguise their Haitian ethnicity and Creole language proficiency to assimilate as African Americans. The musical tastes of this kind of group would say much of sociological interest concerning generational differences in the Haitian community but would fall outside of a study examining "Haitian music" in the diaspora. What I am pointing to here is the gulf between adequate reception studies (that could honestly make some representation about "community" tastes and preferences using quantitative methods) and genre and performance-based studies that sometimes make those kinds of representations but with little methodological justification.

4. In part because Tabou Combo's song and album titles so neatly dovetail with the members'perception of their situation, I name my sections after Tabou Combo albums.

5. Based in part on the profile of the Tabou Combo song "Junior" (Boncy 1992, 121-124).

6. Boncy (1992, 124) claims that the name was a veiled reference to the political troubles of the period, specifically to the many secretive movements of the Tonton Makout in their neighborhood (which housed both a Makout headquarters and police station).

7. According to Alix Pascal (1988): "Herman Nau from Tabou Combo, he introduces the half-Rara. Rara is 'tin ti-din tin' (quarter, eighth, dotted quarter, quarter notes) and he left out that eighth note so it goes 'tim-tim-tim' (two dotted quarters and a quarter note). And he was playing a straight four beat (on the bass drum) long before disco music. He had a lot of influence on mini-jazz and on the whole Caribbean."

The term "Rara" refers to the peasant societies that parade through the countryside in the period between Carnival and Easter. Rara instruments include single-note bamboo trumpets (*vaksin*-s), tin horns, and a variety of drums, rattles, and scraped instruments. The groups are linked philosophically to Vodou and their activities are considered sacred obligations, despite the generally exuberant and ribald atmosphere of the processions. Along with the music of Vodou ceremonies, Rara music is considered one of the most representative Afro-Haitian forms.

8. The line-up of personnel in the band at the time of the recording was Albert Chancy, guitar and maestro; Adolph "Ti-Dòf"

Chancy, bass; Herman Nau, drums; Jean Yves "Fanfan Ti-Bòt"
Joseph, congas; Jean-Claude Jean, rhythm guitar; Yvon "Kapi"
André, bell and tamtam; Paul Gonnel, accordion; Roger M.
"Shoubou" Etienne, vocals; Serge Guerrier, vocals; and Fritz
Coulanges (guest musician), violin.

9. The term "cacos" referred to armed peasant bands in Haiti at
the turn of the century which fought in the service of one or
another presidential hopefuls and which later took up arms
against the U.S. Marines during the occupation of 1915-1934.

10. "Respect," on *Respect*, Mini Records MRS 1039, recorded by
Tabou Combo, 1972-73.

11. Some of the responsibility for the traditional gestures in the
music was attributable to the influence of music advisor Alix
Pascal, who encouraged the group to experiment with more Haitian folk rhythms and roots music. The band, however, remained
divided over the place of roots music in its overall musical formula, and Pascal was disappointed that *The Masters* was not
the Rara-roots album he envisioned.

12. With their adoption of this look, Tabou Combo aligned themselves with African-American musical ensembles of the 1970s
that were exploring the concept of futuristic escape and the lib-
erating potential of sci-fi. Included in this movement of African-American sci-fi semiotics were experimental and marginal
projects like Sun Ra's *Arkestra* and the early hip hop of Afrika
Bambaataa and more mainstream groups like Tower of Power
and even the Commodores.

13. The chord progression of the chorus of "Respect" (Im-V7, a common one for konpa) changed to a major I-IV-V7 for a more
melodic bridge section (the *chanjman* or change). "Zapaton/Re-
spect" recycled the chorus without the "Respect" verses. Three
albums later (*The Music Machine*), the chorus reappeared as
"Mabouya." A *mabouya* is the largest lizard in Haiti and because of its loping gait, its name has been used to characterize
the figure-eight motion of the hips in Haitian dance, also known
as *gwiyad*. In "Mabouya," Etienne sang *"Fanm nan danse kon
mabouya"* ("The woman dances like a lizard"), and a distinctive, rooster-like chorus "Ki-ki-li-ki-ki-li-ki-ki" was added to the
minor chord section.

In 1982, an early version of the French Antillean band Kassav, called
Sokoué Kô Ou, released the album *Vacances* with a zouk-like
medley combining Tabou Combo's "Mabouya" with some material from Tabou's "Light Is Coming Your Way," ("Eee-pip-pip,
eee-pip-pip"). The result was one of the group's first hits, "New
York City Amelioré" ("New York City Improved"). In 1989, the
French producers who had put together the pseudo-Brazilian
band Kaoma that launched the short-lived lambada craze, released a follow-up to their gold record *World Beat* (Epic 46016)
called *Lambada* (Epic 46052, 1990). On it, rising lambada star
Betto Douglas sang a song credited to him and F. Arthur called
"Lambada do Galo Galo," a note-for-note steal of Kassav's med-
ley of Tabou Combo hits centered around "Mabouya" but with
no credit to Tabou Combo or even to Kassav. In 1995, a Tabou
Combo spin-off band called Kolaj, led by Jean-Yves Joseph and
Yves Abel, capped off their debut album with a "Tabou Combo
Medley" reprising Kassav's "New York City Amelioré" once more.

14. "Hommage à Nemours Jean-Baptiste," on *Baissez-Bas*, Tabou
Combo LP 7985, recorded by Tabou Combo, 1980.

15. This history is dealt with in detail in Guilbault et al (1993).

16. "Konpa M Se Pa M," on *Aux Antilles*, Zafem Records TCLP 8056,
recorded by Tabou Combo, 1988.

17. "Go Tabou Go!," on *Go Tabou Go!*, Mini Records MRS 2568,
recorded by Tabou Combo, 1993.

REFERENCES CITED

André, Yvon. 1987. Interview with CC Smith and Gérard Tacite
Lamothe.
_____.1989. Personal interview with author.
Averill, Gage. 1990. "Tabou Combo: Brooklyn's Bridge to the Carib-
bean," *The Beat* 9(4): 27-31, 39, 62.
_____.1995. "'*Mezanmi, Kouman Nou Ye?* My Friends, How Are You?'
Musical Constructions of the Haitian Transnation." *Diaspora, A
Journal of Transnational Studies* 3(3): 253-272.
Boncy, Ralph. 1992. *La chanson d'Haïti, Tome 1: 1965-1985*. Québec:
CIDIHCA.
Buchanan, Susan Huelsebus. 1980. "Scattered Seeds: The Meaning
of the Migration for Haitians in New York City." Ph.D. disserta-
tion, New York University.

Denis, Robert "Bobby. " 1988. Personal interview with author.

Franck, Ricardo "Ti-Plume." 1993. Personal interview with author.

Guilbault, Jocelyne, with Gage Averill, Edouard Benoit, and Gregory Rabess. 1993. *Zouk: World Music in the West Indies*. Chicago: University of Chicago Press.

Joseph, Jean-Yves. 1989. Personal interview with author.

Laguerre, Michèl S. 1984. *American Odyssey: Haitians in New York City*. Ithaca: Cornell University Press.

Nau, Herman. 1985. "Mise au point du Tabou Combo." *Haïti-Observateur*, September 20-27, p. 17.

Pascal, Alix "Tit." 1988. Personal interview with author.

Pasquet, André "Dadou." 1988. Personal interview with author.

Paul, Fred. 1991. Personal interview with author.

Rainer, Ed. 1994. "Duel Phantoms-Tabou: Kino et Shoubou en parlant," *Haïti-Progrès*, May 25-31, p. 18-19.

Schiller, Nina Glick, Josh DeWind, Marie Lucie Brutus, Carolle Charles, Georges Fouron, and Antoine Thomas. 1987. "All in the Same Boat? Unity and Diversity in Haitian Organizing in New York." In *Caribbean Life in New York City: Sociocultural Dimensions*, eds. Constance Sutton and Elsa M. Chaney, 181-201. Staten Island, NY: Center for Migration Studies of New York, Inc.

TABOU COMBO DISCOGRAPHY

Haïti (1969); Ibo Records ILP-146

Disque Souvenir de Tabou Combo. (1970, no catalogue number)

Tabou Combo à La Canne à Sucre (1971); Rotel Records

Respect (1972-3); Mini Records MRS 1039

8th Sacrament (1974); Mini Records MRS 1044

The Masters (1975); Mini Records

Indestructible (1976); Mini Records

L'An X (1977); Rotel Records

Moving the Big Apple (1977); Unreleased demo

Tabou Mania (1978); Mini Records MRS1070

The Music Machine (1978); Mini Records MRS 1070

Voye Monte (1979); Tabou Combo Records and Tapes TCLP 7975

Baissez-Bas (1980); TCLP 7985

Panama Querida (1981); TCLP 7995

Ce Konsa Ce Konsa (1982); TCLP 8015

Men Sirop (1983); TCLP 8025

Jucy Lucy—Jalousie (1985); TCLP 8035

Incident (1986); TCLP 8045

Kitem Fe Zafem (1987); TCLP 8055

Aux Antilles (1988); Zafem Records TCLP 8056
Live aux Zenith, Les Plus Grandes Succès (1989); Zafem Records
     TCLP 8057
Zap Zap (1991); Zafem Records TCLP 8058
Tabou Combo 1979-1986 Vols.1-5 (1992); Mini Records
Go Tabou Go! (1993); Mini Records MRS 2568
Rasanble (1994); Zafem Records TCLP 8059, also *Unity* (1994),
     Hibiscus Records.
Réference (1985); Nouvèl Jenerasyon Records NJ 116

The Changing Hats of Haitian Staged Folklore in New York

Lois Wilcken

The meanings that people invest in music and dance are dynamic, changing through time and across space. When people in Port-au-Prince adapted Haitian folklore for the modern stage fifty years ago, they were responding to specific interests. Staged folklore continues its development in Port-au-Prince and New York, but for different reasons, addressing changing sets of concerns. This essay traces the evolution of meaning invested in staged folklore among Haitian immigrants in New York.

What is Haitian folklore? Most broadly, it refers to Haiti's popular culture. But the word "folklore" entered Haitian discourse in the context of nationalist movements in the early twentieth century. For the upper class and the black intelligentsia who promoted it, literature and theater provided the best vehicles for folklore, and they created a national theater for the purpose of representation. While folklore has its roots in folk tradition, its proponents have adapted it for the modern stage.

For the sake of contextualization, I provide a synopsis of Haitian folk music and dance in traditional settings, followed by an historical overview of Haitian nationalism and its use of expressive culture for self promotion. The remainder of the essay will focus on the migration to New York, the reasons for the continuation of nationalist art, and the gradual change from a nationalist to a multicultural function for staged folklore.

The Traditional Sources of Staged Folklore

The materials of staged folklore in Haiti are rooted in *Vodou* (reverence of spirits), *Kanaval* and *Rara* (Carnival cycle), and the *konbit* (labor cooperative). These nourish the core of the repertory, while dances of European derivation occupy the periphery.[1]

Haitian Vodou stresses serving the *lwa*, spiritual entities that are grouped into *nasyon*-s (nations) deriving from the various peoples of West African and Congolese origin who were enslaved in colonial St. Domingue. Vodou rites preserve the notion of a slave coalition. Each nation has its songs, dances, percussion patterns, instruments, and performance practices. These unfold most spectacularly in a public event called a *dans* (dance), or *seremoni* (ceremony). Servants (*ousi*-s) sing and dance to the accompaniment of a battery of three drums (*maman, segon, boula*) and an iron idiophone (*ogan*) conducted by a master drummer. An officiating priest (*ougan*) or priestess (*manbo*) keeps time with a rattle, and a song specialist (*oudjènikon*) leads the congregation in call-and-response singing.

The percussion ensemble pattern is woven from those of the three drums, the ogan, and the rattle. A slow pulse underlies the pattern. The *kase* (pronounced kah-say) of Vodou drumming counters the regularity of the basic pulse. Derived from the French for "to break," it is a pattern played by the master drummer, signalling the dancers to perform a movement also called a kase. Because it is oppositional to the main pattern, the kase effects a feeling of rupture that brings the spirit to a servant's head.

As each nation has its own rhythm, so does each have its own characteristic dance movement. Vodou dances mimic the spirits. For example, *yanvalou* is danced for the Rada spirits, whose central figure Danbala rises from the cosmic sea and arches toward the sky in a zigzag movement, thus generating new life. The dance yanvalou expresses Danbala's movement through an undulation of the shoulders and spine.

The festival cycles of Kanaval and Rara are marked by irreverent and licentious behavior, yet they are tied to the Christian calendar and include Vodou rites, such as the baptism of instruments and costumes. For the last thirty years in Port-au-Prince, commercial bands have been the principal attraction of these festivals, but folkoric dance companies base their representations on the classic, traditional Carnival.

Kanaval groups traditionally include stilt-walkers, maypole dancers, jugglers, men dressed as women, and caricatures of military and civil authorities. The positions of highest rank are filled by members of the Kanaval band. In general, the band features a corps of singers (with a soloist), trumpets, saxophones, cornets, drums, tambourines, and an assortment of gongs, rattles, and scrapers.

Some of the rhythms of Kanaval accompany specific dances, for example, *maskawon* and *rabòdaj*. Other rhythms are taken from Vodou.

Kanaval segues into Rara. The Rara band is directed by its *prezidan* (president) or *kolonèl* (colonel), often with the assistance of a *majè* (major). The instrumentation of the Rara band is distinguished from that of Kanaval chiefly by a battery of three to five variously pitched bamboo trumpets called *vaksin*-s. The drum battery, called maskawon after one of the dances, includes a large conical drum, a tambourine (*bas*), and a small drum that marks time (*kata*). The chorus of female singers is led by a soloist called a *sanba*. The dances include Rara, rabòdaj, *chay o pie*, maskawon, and several Vodou dances, notably *petwo*.

Collective labor associations called konbit provide further source material for staged folklore. The konbit may gather for activities that would benefit from cooperative effort, like tilling the fields and coffee sorting. Song leaders called sanba or *simidò* and musicians with drums, trumpets, vaksin-s, conch shells, and hoe blades struck with stones signal the konbit in the early morning hours and accompany work movement throughout the day. The sanba and workers sing in call-and-response form. The rhythms of the konbit derive from rural dances, including *djouba*, the Vodou dance of the earth lwa. The traditional konbit culminates in a song, dance, and drinking party.

The dances of Vodou, Kanaval, Rara, and the konbit are the backbone of staged folklore in Haiti and in the Haitian diaspora. This repertory, or collection, of folk songs and dances presumably marks identity for Haitian people. But as James Clifford observed, when folklore is collected and preserved as a domain of identity, "It is tied up with nationalist politics, with restrictive law, and with contested encodings of past and future" (1988, 218). A fervent nationalist debate with ideological, political, and cultural dimensions accompanied folklore to the modern stage in Haiti.

Contested Encodings: Haitian Nationalism

Nationalism is an effort to forge a collective identity based on common origin, history, or language. It obscures other bases of identity, such as class. Types of nationalism vary according to social and historical circumstances, but in colonized (and neo-colonized) societies, nationalists are typically privileged people who call on all classes to defend "the nation" against the colonizer. As we shall see, expressive culture plays a crucial role in the evolution and propagation of nationalism.

Haitian nationalism has a long history.[2] The nation-state of Haiti, formerly the French colony of St. Domingue, was born of the collaborative struggle of enslaved Blacks for freedom, and of freed mulattos for independence from France. But after the Revolution (1791-1804), the class and cultural traits that distinguished the collaborators shaped a bi-polar society. The former slaves emulated African models of belief and socio-economic organization (worship of ancestral spirits, cooperative labor, decentralized economy) while the new mulatto elites followed models from Europe (Roman Catholicism, bourgeois form of government, dependence on foreign capital).

Haiti's position of dependence in the capitalist world, the racism that rationalizes that dependence, and the class stratification of the society are all conditions for the development of persistent contradictions. Incongruities, for example, mark the attitudes of Haitian leaders and intellectuals toward the masses. The ruling class has defended all Haitian citizens as progressives because they defeated imperial France (Price 1900, 524), yet they regard the neo-African culture of the masses as backward, superstitious, and a cause for embarrassment (Innocent 1935 [1906], 157). Haitian elites have attempted, through ruthless "anti-superstition" campaigns, to inculcate their values in the peasantry. Despite their claims to modernity, however, elites actually impose a feudal mode of socio-economic organization on the masses, and elements of their Roman Catholicism are at odds with modern values.

Contradictions are equally apparent in the attitudes that Haitians of all classes take toward their blackness. These attitudes often appear as a vacillating love-hate relationship with Africa. Melville Herskovits was the first scholar to comment on what he named "socialized ambivalence" in Haiti. Calling it a "fundamental clash of custom within the culture...responsible for the *many shifts in allegiance* that continually take place..." (1937, 295; emphasis added), he attributed ambivalence to incongruous African and European elements in Haitian culture. Others have observed ambivalence while interpreting it differently (Bourguignon 1969; Buchanan 1980), but none has recognized that ambivalence waxes in the absence of a strongly critical discourse on race and class.[3]

The first United States invasion and occupation of Haiti (1915-34) kindled a discourse on race among the elites whose interests would suffer under the North American program for the modernization of Haiti. This discourse provided the foundation for a nationalist movement, the expressive dimension of which was the "indigenist" movement in literature and music. For the first time,

Haitian elites valorized Haiti's African roots as a tool for claiming superiority over North Americans—and as a means of eliciting the support of the masses. Jean Price-Mars, who in 1928 wrote the first ethnography of Haiti's masses, imaginatively captured these sentiments:

> ...we remember our race, which the Yankee qualifies as inferior and treats with disdain. Reaching back to the most distant past, we confront our origins again. We adopt...a certain pride in calling ourselves black. Africa is engulfed in our prose, its nostalgia enfolded in our poems, like the breeze in the sails of the caravel on which we embark with our bartered dreams. The word "folklore" thunders into our vocabulary (quoted in Cornevin 1973, 13; author's translation).

Price-Mars, who introduced the word "folklore" into Haitian intellectual discourse, took it from the French scholar Sébillot, who took it from its British inventor William Thoms. Clearly, "folklore" is an ideologically pregnant term in Haiti.

The political crisis precipitated by the 1915 invasion by the United States galvanized the nationalist movement. Elites appealed to middle- and working-class Blacks who also suffered from the subsequent nineteen-year occupation. A cross-class coalition elected Sténio Vincent, a mulatto elite, to the presidency. Vincent was a nationalist, and he brought the occupation to an end ahead of schedule. After the North American troops left in 1934, however, his mulatto elite government reneged on its promises of assistance to the middle and working classes, and a struggle for power based on class and race ensued.

A faction of middle-class Haitians developed a black nationalism riddled with its own contradictions. More radical than the elites, black nationalists romanticized the "primitive" in countless poems, novels, and dramas crafted in the style of European surrealism. The writings of the Griots, a wing of the movement that promoted racial theories, venerated Vodou. Listen to the words of Lorimer Denis and François "Papa Doc" Duvalier:

> The mentality of the black African is profoundly and essentially mystical...the African is the most religious of peoples....An eminently spiritual character puts [African civilizations] in opposition to the positivist utilitarianism of white culture (Denis and Duvalier, 1936, 15-16; author's translation).

Despite these sentiments, Denis and Duvalier situated the "spiritual movement of the Griots in the current of modern humanism" (Denis and Duvalier 1940, 621; author's translation). These contradictions might explain, in part, why black nationalism failed to bring about social change for Haiti's masses.

In summary, nationalism follows a distinct pattern in Haiti. In each of its manifestations—the Haitian Revolution, elite resistance to North American occupation, black resistance to mulatto control—relatively privileged people directed the movement. They elicited the solidarity of the masses, then dissolved their coalition on meeting their own needs. Haitian nationalism failed for the majority of the people because it constructed an identity that ignored class (Depestre 1980, 82-83) while masking rather than addressing the persistent problem of ambivalence. These forces have had their analogues in expressive culture, for as black nationalism ripened so did staged folklore.

The Cultural Dimension: Staged Folklore

Expressive culture played an active role in promoting Haitian nationalism. Elite composers such as Justin Elie and Werner Jaegerhuber were trained abroad and emulated European nationalists by writing sonatas and rondos based on Haitian folk tunes and dance rhythms. To distinguish themselves, black nationalists developed a style they named *foklò* (folklore) because it was presumably more firmly rooted in peasant culture than the nationalist art of the elites. Nonetheless, they tailored their representations to the modern stage.

Staged folklore originated during the same decade that black nationalists come into power. Lina Blanchet, a classical music instructor, attracted interest in 1939 with her arrangements of folk songs for Haiti Chante (Haiti Sings), a chorus she directed (Yarborough 1959, 3). In 1941, writer Jacques Roumain established the Bureau d'Ethnologie to conduct research into the African and Amerindian roots of Haitian culture. The Bureau brought peasant informants into Port-au-Prince to demonstrate music and dance for students of ethnology, and it organized a chorus with the unlikely name of Mater Dolorosa to perform Vodou songs and dances at scholarly conferences. Jean Léon Destiné, a member of the Blanchet choir, took courses at the Bureau, then choreographed peasant dances for his group, now called Haiti Chante et Danse (Haiti Sings and Dances) (Destiné 1990).

Staged folklore responded to international forces as well as local. Troupes that performed folk music and dance in other countries contributed to the modeling of Blanchet's group and Mater Dolorosa. In 1943 Haitian representatives traveled to Panama for an Assembly of Ministers and Directors of Education of the American Republics, and they later reprinted the Assembly's resolution in the *Bulletin* of the Bureau of Ethnology. The following is an excerpt:

> Resolved that each nation intensify folkloric studies by means of public and private research institutes...that diplomatic representatives aid in the development of artistic programs in state theaters where interpretive groups exhibit the best folkloric expression of the countries they represent...(Anon. 1947, 37-38; author's translation).

In 1949, the black nationalist government of Dumarsais Estimé created La Troupe Folklorique Nationale to represent Haiti in the new state theater and abroad.

No filmed documents of staged folklore remain from this early period, but two books published in the 1950s provide useful description and photographs. In 1955 the Bureau of Ethnology published Michel Lamartinière Honorat's ethnography, which classifies the folk dances and discusses musical instruments and melodies. The body of his book describes the principal dances of Vodou, as well as the "profane" dances of Kanaval, Rara, the konbit, and Europe (minuet, contradance, lancier). The author used many photographs from the collection of the Bureau of Ethnology that featured the dancers of Mater Dolorosa and other troupes. In his introduction, Honorat captured the spirit of a performance by La Troupe Macaya:

> The spectacle was truly moving and spirited. The thunder of applause that greeted each rise and fall of the curtain underscored the perfect communion of spirit of the spectators, the artists, and the art itself. The joy—I would almost say the delirium—of the multi-colored crowd, which tossed men, women, and children together in an agitated mass, like the sea, led me to observe and analyze how human psychology awakens when it finds itself in the presence of that which it apprehends immediately, that which it understands without deep reflection, as integral to its own nature (Honorat 1955, 9; author's translation).

The late African-American dancer Lavinia Williams used the repertoire of the national troupe to structure her book *Haiti-Dance*

(1959). Williams was working with Katherine Dunham's company in New York in 1953 when the Bureau of Tourism of the government of President Paul Magloire (1950-56) hired her to train members of the national troupe. She subsequently made her life in Port-au-Prince, with an occasional visit to New York to perform and train dancers. In her book Williams counted and described a total of forty-one pieces in the national troupe's repertoire. Twenty-four of them are Vodou dances: fifteen compositions based on dance movement and nine dramatizations of ritual. Williams named three Carnival dances, five dances of the konbit, one "dance of diversion," five dances of European derivation, and three choreographies with a pronounced "modern" influence.

The modern influence is apparent in all of staged folklore, even while folklore aims to establish popular authenticity. Many poor and working-class Haitians have played in the troupes because of their ability to drum or sing, but middle- and upper-class personnel have made the artistic decisions. The distinctive foklò composition, the *koréografi* (choreography), fuses traditional and modern elements. The Vodou ritual drum battery serves as the model for the staged folklore music ensemble, but some troupes include horns and electric amplification. To this accompaniment, a corps modeled after the *corps de ballet* elaborates basic Afro-Haitian dance, creating new variations on traditional movement while outlining set floor designs. A representative choreography might begin with the following:

Step	# of Ogan Patterns (duration)	Floor design
1	16	Entrance from wings V-formation
Kase 1	4	Diamond
2	8	Diamond to opposing lines
Kase 2	8	Two lines merge into one
Etc.	...	...

Figure 1. Opening structure of a hypothetical choreography.

Notice that choreographies use the kase, but the function of the kase, which is spiritual in the temple, is formal on stage. In other words, the unforeseeable psycho-social dynamics of the congregation determine points of kase in the temple, while the demands of four-square design determine them in compositions for the stage.

Folklore troupes enjoyed a heyday during the regimes of Dumarsais Estimé and Paul Magloire (1946-56). It is one of the ironies of Haitian cultural history that this epoch came to an end when François Duvalier rose to power in 1957, because Duvalier had been one of the more radical proponents of black nationalism. The political economy of Duvalierism was predatory, even for his own class (the black petty bourgeoisie), and it triggered massive emigration, especially to New York City.

New York, Phase One: Staging Folklore in the Diaspora

The dynasty of François "Papa Doc" Duvalier (1957-71) and his son Jean-Claude "Baby Doc" Duvalier (1971-86) repeated the pattern of other nationalist movements in Haiti. The first Haitians to flee the dictatorship were elites menaced by Papa Doc's anti-mulatto stance, but the Duvaliers gradually came to a comfortable alliance with the traditional elites (Dupuy 1989, 164), a compact that betrayed the interests of the black middle-class as well as those of the masses whose culture Papa Doc had championed. The diaspora gained momentum in the 1970s with the chain migration of middle-class Haitians, and by the 1980s many poorer Haitians were finding ways to enter New York.

The migration to the United States swept up a substantial number of folklore artists, and they were quick to establish companies in New York. When the national folklore troupe was formed in 1949, its choreographers were Jean Léon Destiné, André Narcisse, André Germain, and Louinès Louinis (Yarborough 1959, 7). All but Narcisse came to New York and established troupes named after themselves.

Jean Léon Destiné considered himself an "ambassador" of Haitian arts, settling in New York long before Duvalier came to power. He had performed with Lina Blanchet's group at a pan-American conference in Washington, D.C., in 1941. Inspired by the gathering's internationally renowned African and African-American dancers, Destiné was determined to go to New York, and his opportunity came by way of a scholarship to study printing. His career in printing fell by the wayside when he attracted the interest and support of such artists as Pearl Primus and Katherine Dunham. Destiné found a job in the Education Department of New York's American Museum of Natural History. Collaborating with Barbadian dancer Jeanne Raymond, Haitian drummer Alphonse Cimber, and a professional manager, he established himself as a teacher and a performer. Destiné added dancers to this core over time, and the group made itself known through the Museum. Initially, his audience was not Haitian, because a community scarcely existed in New York in the 1940s. In 1949 he returned to Port-au-Prince to form the national folkloric troupe, but he maintained a base in New York. As Haitians entered New York in massive numbers during the Duvalier years, Destiné secured a place in their festivals (Destiné 1990).

Louinès Louinis was among the artists who performed at the Bureau of Ethnology during the 1940s. In 1949, when Destiné formed the national dance company, he joined as choreographer. Louinis became fully aware of the artistic potential of staged folklore when he traveled to Havana with the Haitian national troupe in the early 1950s and saw a performance of a Cuban troupe. He immigrated to New York in 1972 and studied dance with a scholarship from New Dance Group in Manhattan, where Destiné taught a class. Louinis substituted for Destiné when the latter toured outside New York, and eventually built his own company out of New Dance Group students. Initially, none of his group was Haitian, but as he played increasingly for Haitian community festivals, he attracted Haitian-born artists, until the entire troupe was Haitian. Louinis' troupe had a strong presence at Brooklyn College, where Haitians produced their most impressive festivals in the 1970s and 1980s (Louinis 1990).

The Ibo Dancers were formed in 1968 on the initiative of Ermile St. Lot, a young Haitian student at Brandeis High School in Manhattan. St. Lot organized his group for a school performance featuring ethnic clubs. The dancers won the recognition of the Haitian Neighborhood Service Center, a community organization that presented the group to Haitian audiences. St. Lot was the grandson of a black nationalist orator, and the nephew of Paulette St. Lot, who had promoted Haitian folklore through her position with Haiti's Bureau of Tourism. Paulette became the choreographer and artistic director of the Ibo Dancers, accompanying their numbers with traditional songs. The Ibo Dancers received funds in 1969 from the Community Development Agency, a Division of New York City's Human Resource Administration, and consequently secured a contract with the New York City Parks Department. The company was a strong presence in the immigrant community during the 1970s and 1980s (St. Lot 1990).

Ibo Dancers on stage at Brooklyn College, 1981. Photo by Lois Wilcken.

Arnold Elie began his career in folklore in 1947, when he danced for La Troupe Folklorique Macaya. From Macaya he joined the national company (he appears in several of the photographs that illustrate Williams' book). Elie migrated to the Bahamas in 1962, possibly in flight from the Haitian dictatorship, and entered New York in 1969. He created costumes and an occasional choreography for the chorus Troupe Choucoune until 1972 when he founded his own troupe and named it after Shango, the Nigerian thunder god. Troupe Shango enjoyed equal exposure to the Haitian festival audience with Destiné, the Ibo Dancers, and Louinès Louinis during the 1970s and 1980s. Because Elie was a professional tailor, his costumes were the most brilliant, although they revealed his inclination toward camp. He was a Vodou priest as well and officiated over rituals in his Flatbush apartment (Elie 1988). When Elie passed away in 1990, Vodouists and folklore artists drummed and sang at his graveside in folkloric costume.

Twoup Konbit made its debut in the early 1980s as a youth choral group based in St. Augustine's Roman Catholic Church in Park Slope, Brooklyn. Most of its members were second-generation Haitian Americans inspired by liberation theology. Taking advantage of state funds, the church arranged for Louinis and Destiné to train the members in dance. The group named itself Twoup Konbit after the Haitian rural labor collective, and spelled its name in Creole to signify a feeling of solidarity with the masses. Konbit worked in the parishes of exiled priests, and performed with the progressive theater group Kalfou Lakay (Crossroads of the House), reinterpreting traditional dances in the context of the anti-Duvalierism struggle and dramatizing the problem of the Haitian boat people. Twoup Konbit disbanded in the early 1990s, but director Marie Edith Jean created a new children's group, Tonel Lakay (Arbor of the House, a reference to the rural Vodou dance floor), based in St. Augustine's parish (Twoup Konbit 1989).

Did the change of context—Port-au-Prince to New York—change the style of staged folklore? The five profiles show that individuals who were not Haitian performed in the companies, and one company was almost entirely second generation. These individuals introduced details of movement characteristic of "foreign" style, such as jazz and modern. However, this also happened in Port-au-Prince, although to a lesser extent. The profiles also show that non-Haitian institutions provided venues for staged folklore. Because many of these institutions served minorities and saw Haitians as black, Haitian groups in New York rarely performed the aforementioned European choreographies that Honorat and Williams documented in the 1950s. These changes were relatively minor. The choreography maintained its place as the preferred form of representation, and the drum ensemble music of Vodou and other Afro-Haitian traditions remained the preferred accompaniment in New York. Most important, New York's Haitian community created the festival, a context for staged folklore that encouraged stylistic conservatism.

Newspaper editor Firmin Joseph originated the festival presentation format. His festivals were essentially variety shows, with commercial bands, folklore troupes, comedians, raffles, and awards. Among venues, Joseph preferred Whitman Hall at Brooklyn College in Flatbush. Other individuals and organizations used his model to present smaller-scale festivals in high school and church auditoriums. The festival was for those "nostalgic of Haiti," Joseph said, to "remind them of home" (1983).

Joseph was a black nationalist. In 1983 I worked for his newspaper and observed his promotion of the ideology through the print medium. An excerpt from the following review of a troupe in Joseph's newspaper is reminiscent of an earlier quote from Griots Denis and Duvalier, where black spirituality is contrasted with the materialism of "white" culture:

> Perpetuating the essence and the highest expression of the popular culture has always been a drama for emigré artists— above all, in an environment where it is easy to lose one's identity, to become alienated in a materialistic civilization where the sacred gesture has no place and where the dance is

only a caricature of mechanistic society (Anon. 1982, 16; author's translation).

Joseph's festival programs always included the folklore troupe—sometimes two or three—as the expression of Afro-Haitian identity. But incongruities troubled this apparent support. Joseph's meager fee for staged folklore ($200 per company per performance) discouraged artists. When he was murdered in September 1983—the reasons are still obscure—the large-scale festival virtually died with him.

Haitians continued to produce nationalist art in New York, even while the black nationalist government in Port-au-Prince was in disrepute. This paradox owes partly to the persistence of cultural patterns; partly, as Joseph himself had pointed out, to the nostalgia of Haitian immigrants; and partly to the availability of funds to promote New York City's cultural pluralism (a foreshadowing of the multicultural movement in the 1990s). But the fall of the Duvalier dynasty signalled change. As black nationalism waned, so did staged folklore.

New York, Phase Two:
Class, Race, and Ambivalence

In the 1980s the class character of the Haitian diaspora to New York changed. Deep corruption and the failure of Jean-Claude Duvalier's neoliberal economy based on offshore assembly—the manufacture of Haitian goods for export using technology and materials imported from the United States—were driving a greater number of working-class Haitians into New York even before the regime fell in 1986. Many of the new immigrants moved into Brownsville, East Flatbush, and other impoverished New York neighborhoods. The folkloric artists among them found little support within the Haitian community. They either abandoned their art, or turned toward outside sources of support. The story of one company, La Troupe Makandal, serves as a paradigm for these changes.

A group of teenagers from Belair, a poor and working-class quarter of Port-au-Prince, founded La Troupe Makandal in 1973. They learned dance and music in the Vodou houses of Belair, and were aware of the story of Makandal, a hero of the Haitian Revolution. Although they were not from the black intelligentsia that promoted nationalism, staged folklore appealed to them, partly because it offered a way out of a life of assembly labor. Using costumes that they fabricated from paper, they organized neighborhood performances called *wol*. Because their namesake, Makandal, is known in Vodou myth as a magician, they built their choreographies on the idea of magic, with members eating fire and dancing on broken glass. They distinguished themselves enough to find work and continue their development.

La Troupe Makandal arrived in New York in 1981 following specific changes in United States-Haiti relations. The Carter administration had pressured the Haitian government to liberalize politically as well as economically. A free press and political parties were forming when Ronald Reagan replaced Carter. Reagan's election signalled an anti-liberal crackdown on the part of the Duvalier dictatorship in November 1980. Political dissidents were the first to flee, but massive numbers of working-class Haitians followed. An official of the United States Embassy in Port-au-Prince told me that more than 350 people left Haiti through dance companies in 1981. La Troupe Makandal was one of those companies.

The members of Makandal were not part of the chain migration that brought the middle class to the United States. They had no family in New York, and they procured their visas not through purchase but on the strength of their artistic talent. When they arrived in New York in the fall of 1981, they crowded into two unheated basement rooms in a poor neighborhood of East Flatbush, Brooklyn. Their new neighborhood teemed with working-class Haitians, many living, like themselves, in illegal basement space.

Makandal connected with the artistic community though Frisner Augustin, a master drummer who had entered New York in 1972. Like the members of Makandal, Augustin experienced poverty in Haiti. And like many Vodou drummers, he used staged folklore as a way out of that poverty.[4] Through the 1970s the immigrant community heard him play for the folklore troupes in festivals. When Makandal entered in 1981, Augustin was living several blocks away from them, so their meeting him was fortuitous. Augustin wanted to form his own troupe—a rarity for a drummer because dancers directed most of the companies. He took Makandal under his wing and introduced them to Firmin Joseph. One month after their arrival in New York, they played in a Thanksgiving Day festival at Brooklyn College.

The essentially middle-class audience that saw Makandal perform at Brooklyn College and elsewhere in the community during its first year in New York considered the troupe sensational and risqué, and this reception influenced the group's repertory and performance style. Makandal distinguished itself from other folklore companies in New York by a repertory that revealed the elements of Vodou most strongly suggestive of black magic, primitive sensuality, and, by association, Haiti's impoverishment. One of the dancers rendered

La Troupe Makandal on stage at Brooklyn College, circa 1986.
Photo by Chantal Regnault.

a convincing *banda*, the dance of *Gede* (pronounced Gay-day), lord of the cemetery, decay, and resurrection. Gede caricatures human sexuality, and Makandal's Gede, a Vodouist frequently possessed by the spirit, played the role brilliantly. Audiences were demanding "Banda!" whenever Makandal appeared. Augustin interpreted this response as prurient interest and lack of respect for Vodou. Less than a year into Makandal's tenure in New York, he was withdrawing the sensational choreographies from the troupe's repertory and replacing them with more restrained fare.

Economic pressures rapidly altered the group's composition. After its first difficult winter in an unheated basement, one member died, and another started on a path toward alcoholism and drug abuse. Three others left Makandal for full-time work, one as a cook and the other two as factory workers in New Jersey. Two of the remaining three were sisters who devoted their energies to Vodou in the basement temples of Brooklyn's poorer Haitian neighborhoods. One of the sisters, plus the last dancer, continue to play sporadically with the company. As the original members of the group left, Augustin replaced them, often with black and white North Americans. Most of the latter had experience playing with other Haitian companies in New York, and most had secure day jobs.

The problem of ambivalence was manifested when young Haitians joined Makandal. They had to cope with familial opposition, and some even struggled within themselves. One novice, for example, did not dance whenever the company played in Brooklyn because her involvement with the troupe would become apparent to her father, who saw Vodou as incompatible with his Christian beliefs. A male dancer whose family had rejected Vodou during an infamous "anti-superstition campaign" in the early 1940s claimed that Vodou is inherently "evil," yet it is a deeply rooted component of the Haitian soul:[5]

> When you go to a Vodou ceremony, you [the outsider] don't see the evil. You see a show, a theatrical event. You've got to have the sense to understand what evil is all about...
>   No matter what, you [the Haitian] cannot escape yourself. You really can't. Your story is still with you. Take from where I was to this point, even though my father tried to escape it (Telfort 1990).

A dancer who still works with Makandal tells a story of her mother's conflicting attitudes toward the ougan (Vodou priest), and of her own mixed feelings:

> I remember when I was about six or seven years old, I think I was anemic. And they tried all kinds of herbal medicines, and that didn't work. And my mother, although she was a Catholic, I think she still believed in her roots. She sent me to an ougan. And she wouldn't go. She sent me with my cousin....And I was going to Catholic school then. The nuns found out about it, and I got in a lot of trouble. I was scared of [Vodou]. Because that's all I ever heard. "Voodoo hurts people. Voodoo is for people that are illiterate. Voodoo is not a religion." Even now, I try to teach my mother about Vodou. We have a Makandal record in the house. She won't play it. She won't play it at all. If we start playing the drums, she'll walk away. That's how I grew up. I always thought Vodou was no good (Deats 1989).

Interestingly, this dancer recently argued that Makandal ought to downplay Vodou in its promotional materials.

During the 1980s staged folklore became a weak presence in New York's Haitian community. Surveying the New York-based newspaper *Haiti Observateur* for publicity for folkloric companies reveals a steady decline since 1979 in both the number of performances and the number of groups performing for Haitian audiences (Wilcken 1991, 266-68). At the same time, the records of La Troupe Makandal show a healthy increase in the number of performances sponsored by organizations that were not Haitian. Performance fees from such organizations were significantly higher than the Haitian fees.

In conclusion, staged folklore lost its meaning as nationalist art because nationalist discourse had withered. Class and racial divisions came out of the obscurity that nationalism imposes on them, and these divisions expressed themselves as ambivalence toward the culture of (as Deats expressed it in the quote above) "people that are illiterate." Interest from outside the community sustained several companies until new meanings could develop.

New York, Phase Three: Multiculturalism

Since the late 1980s, certain developments in Haiti and in the United States have generated new forms of support for folklore. In Port-au-Prince, *mizik rasin* (roots music) has drawn on elements of folk music to express Haitians' exhilaration over the uprooting of Duvalierism and prospects for democracy. The *Bouyon Rasin* (Roots Stew) Festival that attracted a spectrum of music groups to Port-au-Prince in 1995 included staged folklore. For some young Haitians in New York, the rasin movement has sparked an interest in folk traditions, but it is not clear whether this interest will translate into support for folk troupes. The multicultural movement, however, has proven a source of concrete financial support for folklore. Most organizations that have hired Makandal since the late 1980s have done so from a multiculturalist position.

Proponents of multiculturalism are not uniform in their understanding of the term. Some stress cultural diversity to such a degree that opponents have made a case for the fragmenting effect of the movement on society. At its best, multiculturalism shows a dialectical relationship between the universal and the particular. Multiculturalists differ from their opponents in rejecting the assumption of the universality of *privileged European* culture. As these ideas are debated, the movement is sweeping through the cultural sectors of North American society.

Education and arts presenting, the two primary areas that support folk artists in the United States today, have been deeply influenced by multiculturalism. In education, multiculturalism is a democratization of the curriculum that "enables students to view concepts, issues, themes, and problems from different perspectives and points of view" (Banks 1994, 26). Educators put multiculturalism into practice by including the perspectives of marginalized groups in the curriculum, and by hiring artists of diverse backgrounds for workshops and performances in the schools. In arts presenting, the programming of folk music and dance is rooted in the efforts of folklorists and ethnomusicologists to bring folk arts to the general public (Baron and Spitzer 1992). Their efforts guided the establishment of government funds, festivals, and presenting institutions that specialize in folk arts. Today, public sector folklorists and ethnomusicologists also work with more established cultural institutions that are attempting to diversify their concert programming.

The educational and cultural agencies that provide the support network for multiculturalism are thus school programs, community groups, museums, libraries, government agencies, and arts presenters who collaborate with local folk artists. In New York, the multicultural network supports the work of several music folklore groups. The Caribbean groups include Los Pleneros de la 21 and Los Afortunados (both Puerto Rican), Asa Dife (Dominican Republic), and La Troupe Makandal and the Louinis Haitian Dance Theater (both Haitian). Examples of non-Caribbean groups are Music from China and Cherish the Ladies (Irish). Since the mid-1980s Makandal and these other groups have performed through such agencies as World Music Institute, the Caribbean Cultural Center, City Lore, Arts Connection, and the borough arts councils; and in such venues as the Brooklyn Children's Museum, the Museum of the City of New York, the Schomburg Library, the American Museum of Natural History, Brooklyn College,[6] and in myriad classrooms from kindergarten through college.

The less theatrical, more educational nature of these new settings induce changes in the structure and style of performance. Speakers interpret for the audiences, and program notes contextualize the pieces performed. For Troupe Makandal, the choreographed approach is yielding to a more intimate style in which musicians and dancers are spontaneous in their interaction with one another and with the audience. The unpredictability and engagement associated with "getting the spirit" temper the four-square phrasing shown in Figure 1 above. The emphasis on such elements of folk music style does not come from a need to sensationalize but rather a need to understand the perspectives of ordinary people.

Beautiful Little Haiti

In March 1996, the Prospect Park Alliance presented a weekend of Haitian arts and crafts in Brooklyn's Prospect Park Picnic House. An assortment of foundations and public agencies funded the event. The initial impulse for the project came from the Lila Wallace-Reader's Digest Fund, which gave a substantial grant to the Alliance on the condition that the latter "get in touch" with the various

communities of people who use the park.[7] Alliance staff has re-
searched the Haitian community's use of the park and is creating a
bridge that would link Haitians with the larger surrounding community.

The weekend, dubbed *"Bel Ti Ayiti"* ("Beautiful Little Haiti"), was
a success in terms of attendance and networking. Its promotional
flyer, printed in English and Creole, said, "Both days will feature
workshops, demonstrations, and an open exchange of *Haitian arts
and ideas.*" A simulated Haitian marketplace provided the context
for performances. Most striking were the strong presence of children, and the role played by Cympal, an organization of young
Haitians, in producing and promoting the weekend for the Alliance.
La Troupe Makandal played, storyteller Lucrece Louisdhon dramatized folk tales with dancers from the Louinès Louinis group, and
musician Papa Jube performed his unique blend of Rara, reggae,
and hip hop.

The rationale for events like Bel Ti Ayiti is that they promote
interracial and intercultural harmony. Haitians living in New York
are no less concerned than others that their children coexist peacefully in a diverse society. Staged folklore takes on new meaning in
this context, celebrating the culture of a group that has survived
racist and classist marginalization. An expression of ordinary people,
staged folklore plays a critical role in the multicultural movement.
Bel Ti Ayiti wears a new hat.

NOTES

1. See Honorat (1955), Wilcken (1992), and Yarborough (1959)
   for descriptions of the dances of Vodou, Kanaval, Rara, and the
   konbit. Note that the European dances (waltz, polka, lancier)
   have all but vanished from the repertory of Haitian folklore
   groups. At most, a company might choreograph *bal des
   affranchis*, a quadrille recalling the freed mulattos of the eighteenth century who identified with French culture. Folklore
   companies stage the *contredanse*, but its association with the
   black peasant has Africanized the dance.

2. Haitian nationalists have left a treasury of literary works. See
   Denis and Duvalier (1936); Firmin (1885); Innocent (1935); Price
   (1900); and Price-Mars (1973). For Haitian critiques of nationalism, see Depestre (1980) and Parti Communiste Haïtien/
   Comité Central (1934). All are available at the Schomburg Library in New York City.

3. "Anti-superstition" campaigns and stereotypes of Vodou in North American popular culture nourish ambivalence. The latter have a long history, but they matured in the United States during its first military occupation of Haiti. Stereotypes provided a rationale for the North American presence, and they continue to justify the economic exploitation of the Haitian worker. The process of stereotyping is clear in such literary works as James Seabrook's *The Magic Island* (1929), and in the films *The White Zombie* (1932), *I Walked with a Zombie* (1946), and *The Serpent and the Rainbow* (1988). Some Haitians respond to stereotyping by dissociating from Vodou.

4. Middle-class Haitians danced for folklore troupes but rarely drummed for them—a pattern that suggests some ambivalence toward Vodou. Choreographers had to scout the Vodou temples for drummers. André Germain, one of the original choreographers of the national troupe mentioned earlier, "discovered" Augustin this way.

5. The dancer was referring to one of the more vicious anti-Vodou programs conducted by the Catholic Church with the complicity of the bourgeois government. Haitians remember the campaign as "la renonce" ("the renunciation"). See Métraux (1972, 335-51) for details.

6. The impact of multiculturalism is apparent in a comparison of two performances from different periods in the same venue. Makandal's first performance in New York took place in November 1981 at a Brooklyn College festival with the financing of Firmin Joseph, and the audience was entirely Haitian. The troupe played there in March 1996 under the auspices of World Music Institute (WMI) and the Brooklyn College Institute for Studies in American Music (ISAM). Funding for the 1996 performance came from the National Endowment for the Arts and the New York State Council on the Arts, both government agencies. The Haitian media worked with WMI and ISAM to publicize the event, and the performance drew a healthy balance of Haitians and others. This collaboration could not have happened in 1981.

7. Janine St. Germain, personal communication, May 1995.

REFERENCES CITED

Anonymous. 1947. Resolution sur le folklore. *Bulletin du Bureau d'Ethnologie* (mars): 37-38.

Anonymous. 1982. Ansy Derose à New York. *La Nouvelle Haiti Tribune* 2(9) (June): 16.

Banks, James A. 1994. *An Introduction to Multicultural Education*. Boston: Allyn and Bacon.

Baron, Robert and Nicholas R. Spitzer, eds. 1992. *Public Folklore*. Washington: Smithsonian Institution Press.

Bourguignon, Erika. 1969. "Haiti et l'ambivalence socialisée: Une reconsidération." *Journal de la Societé des Americanistes* 58: 173-205.

Buchanan, Susan Huelsebus. 1980. "Scattered Seeds: The Meaning of the Migration for Haitians in New York City." Ph.D. dissertation, New York University.

Clifford, James. 1988. *The Predicament of Culture*. Cambridge, MA: Harvard University Press.

Cornevin, Robert. 1973. "Jean Price-Mars (1876-1969)." In Price-Mars, 1973.

Deats, Rose. 9 September 1989. Personal interview by the author.

Denis, Lorimer, and François Duvalier. 1936. "La civilisation Haitienne: Notre mentalité est-elle africaine ou gallolatine?" *Revue de la Société d'Histoire et de Géographie d'Haiti* 7(23) (May): 1-31.

Depestre, René. 1980. *Bonjour et adieu à la négritude: Suivi de travaux d'identité*. Paris: Editions Robert Laffont, S.A.

Destiné, Jean Léon. 10 October 1990. Personal interview by the author.

Dupuy, Alex. 1989. *Haiti in the World Economy: Class, Race, and Underdevelopment since 1700*. Boulder and London: Westview Press.

Elie, Arnold. 7 December 1988. Personal interview by the author.

Firmin, Antenor. 1885. *De l'égalité des races humaines (anthropologie positive)*. Paris: F. Pichon.

Herkovits, Melville J. 1937. *Life in a Haitian Valley*. New York: Alfred A. Knopf.

Honorat, Michel Lamartinière. 1955. *Les danses folkloriques Haitiennes*. Publication of the Bureau of Ethnology of the Republic of Haiti, Series II, No. 11. Port-au-Prince: Imprimerie de l'Etat.

Innocent, Antoine. 1935. *Mimola, ou, l'histoire d'une cassette. Petit tableau de moeurs locales*. Original edition, Port-au-Prince: Imprimerie F. Malval, 1906. Port-au-Prince: V. Valcin, Imprimeur.

Joseph, Firmin. July 1983. Personal interview by the author.

Louinis, Louinès. 30 September 1990. Personal interview by the author.

Métraux, Alfred. 1972. *Voodoo in Haiti*. New York: Schocken Books.

Parti Communiste Haïtien/Comité Central. 1934. *Analyse Schématique 32-34*. (Written by Jacques Roumain on behalf of the Party.) Port-au-Prince: V. Valcin.

Price, Hannibal. 1900. *De la réhabilitation de la race noire par la république d'Haiti*. Port-au-Prince: Imprimerie J. Verrollot.

Price-Mars, Jean. 1973. *Ainsi parla l'oncle*. Original edition, Paris: Imprimerie de Compiegne, 1928. Ottawa: Editions Leméac.

Seabrook, William. 1989. *The Magic Island*. Reprint. Originally published New York: Harcourt Brace, 1929. New York: Paragon House.

St. Lot, Ermile. 18 October 1990. Personal interview by the author.

Telfort, Jean. 21 January 1990. Personal interview by the author.

Twoup Konbit. 22 January 1989. Group interview by the author.

Wilcken, Lois. 1991. "Music Folklore Among Haitians in New York: Staged Representations and the Negotiation of Identity." Ph.D. dissertation, Columbia University.

_____. 1992. *The Drums of Vodou*. Tempe, AZ: White Cliffs Media Company.

Yarborough, Lavinia Williams. 1959. *Haiti-Dance*. Frankfurt: Bronners Druckerie.

CONTRIBUTORS

Ray Allen is Acting Director of the Institute for Studies in American Music at Brooklyn College, CUNY, and author of *Singing in the Spirit: African-American Sacred Quartets in New York City* (University of Pennsylvania Press).

Paul Austerlitz is Assistant Professor of Music at Brown University, and author of *Merengue: Dominican Music and Identity* (Temple University Press).

Gage Averill is Associate Professor of Music at New York University and author of *A Day for the Hunter, a Day for the Prey: Popular Music and Power in Haiti* (University of Chicago Press).

Juan Flores is Professor of Black and Puerto Rican Studies at Hunter College, CUNY, and Professor of Sociology and Cultural Studies at the Graduate Center, CUNY. He is author of *Divided Borders: Essays on Puerto Rican Identity* (Arte Público).

Ruth Glasser is a public historian and author of *My Music is My Flag: Puerto Rican Musicians and Their New York Communities, 1917-1940* (University of California Press).

Donald Hill is Professor of Anthropology and Africana/Latino Studies at Oneonta College, SUNY. He is author of *Calypso Calaloo: Early Music in Trinidad* (University Press of Florida).

Philip Kasinitz is Professor of Sociology at Hunter College and the Graduate Center, CUNY, and author of *Caribbean New York: Black Immigrants and the Politics of Race* (Cornell University Press).

Peter Manuel is Professor of Music at John Jay College and the Graduate Center, CUNY, and co-author of *Caribbean Currents: Caribbean Music from Rumba to Reggae* (Temple University Press).

Les Slater is Director of the Trinidad and Tobago Folk Arts Institute in Brooklyn. He is also a journalist, TV producer, and steel pan player.

Lois Wilcken is Adjunct Assistant Professor of Music at Hunter College, CUNY, and an administrative manager at City Lore in New York City. She is author of *The Drums of Vodou* (White Cliffs Media Company).

The University of Illinois Press

is a founding member of the

Association of American University Presses.

University of Illinois Press

1325 South Oak Street

Champaign, IL 61820-6903

www.press.uillinois.edu